The

STRENGTH

OF THE FOUR

The STRENGTH OF THE FOUR

FOUNDATIONS OF INTERGENERATIONAL COMMUNICATION THROUGH THE STORY OF DANIEL

LINDA BROWN & KAITLYN DALLMANN

MEDIA.COM

the
STRENGTH
OF THE FOUR

Scripture quotations, unless otherwise indicated, taken from the New
American Standard Bible®, Copyright © 1960, 1962, 1963, 1968, 1971,
1972, 1973, 1975, 1977, 1995, 2020 by The Lockman Foundation.
Used by permission. (www.lockman.org)

Scripture quotations marked KJV
from the King James Version, public domain.

Scripture quotations marked NIV are taken from the Holy Bible,
New International Version®, NIV®. Copyright © 1973, 1978, 1984, 2011
by Biblica, Inc.™ Used by permission of Zondervan. All rights reserved
worldwide, www.zondervan.com. The "NIV" and "New International
Version" are trademarks registered in the United States Patent
and Trademark Office by Biblica, Inc.™

The views and opinions expressed in this book are those of the author and
do not necessarily reflect the official policy or position of
Illumify Media Global.

Published by
Illumify Media Global
www.IllumifyMedia.com
"Let's bring your book to life!"

Paperback ISBN: 978-1-959099-26-0

Typeset by Art Innovations (http://artinnovations.in/)
Cover design by Debbie Lewis
Internal images by Elena Herzinger - Danigirlsart

Printed in the United States of America

This book is dedicated to my grandchildren:
Kaitlyn, Lauren, Lilia Joy, Elena, Austin, Ethan,
Nash, and Carter.

A Tree Firmly Planted

Blessed is the person who does not walk
in the counsel of the wicked,
Nor stand in the path of sinners,
Nor sit in the seat of scoffers!
But his delight is in the Law of the LORD,
And on His Law he meditates day and night.
He will be like a tree planted by streams of water,
Which yields its fruit in its season,
And its leaf does not wither;
And in whatever he does,
he prospers.

—Psalm 1:1–3

CONTENTS

PREFACE

Welcome to our study of the book of Daniel! A few side notes are important to address before diving into this study. This book was written by both Linda Brown and her granddaughter, Kaitlyn Dallmann. However, for ease in reading, we will indicate which perspective is the focus of each section by labeling it *Linda* or *Kaitlyn*. God gave Linda the inspiration for the project; then, true to the book's theme of intergenerational communication, she and Kaitlyn developed it together.

Throughout, we will be restoring the original Hebrew names of God the Father, God the Son, and God the Holy Spirit. For the purposes of this book, it is important for you to know that God's personal Hebrew name is YHWH, or Yahweh.

The honorific title referring to God in Genesis 1:1 (and over twenty-five hundred other places in the Bible) is Elohim, which can be summarized to mean "the majestic one." In place of the LORD, we may use the name Elohim.

Finally, in place of the name Jesus, we will use Yeshua, which means salvation. It will be helpful for you to become familiar with these names, as they will be used interchangeably throughout this book.

It is also important to note that we will not cover the many prophecies in the book of Daniel. The prophecies of Daniel are extremely important for today and into the future, but the purpose of this book is to evangelize and teach intergenerational communication through the example of Daniel and his three friends.

We do not wish to look down upon other ideas or say ours is the only viewpoint to consider. Only when Yeshua (Jesus) returns will full revelation be revealed. We simply hope that the readers of this book can use the information given to further their walk with the one true God and what He has written in His Word, rather than be offended by a personal opinion or viewpoint. We hope that you search for the truth and accept the guidance of the Holy Spirit, as we have tried to do for this project.

This book is designed to be part book—filled with stories, commentary, and guided information—and part Bible study—filled with reflective questions, fill-in-the-blanks, and "look up this verse" sections. We want this to be very interactive, so please write in this book, highlight things that stick out to you, and use the free spaces to answer questions and capture your thoughts.

Our goal for you, dear reader, is to open conversation and communication among generations. We would love to see grandparents talking about and studying the Word with grandchildren. We would love to see older men and women mentoring and studying with younger generations. We would love to see multigenerational Bible studies in church and homes, asking questions like "What events shaped your generation's upbringing?" and "Why do you see the world the way you do?" and "What does this mean for the body of Yeshua?"

It seems like the parents and grandparents of Daniel and his friends, as well as Jeremiah, a prophet at the time, did a great job of raising a moral and faithful group of young men. The question we should be asking is, "What did they do right?" We should try to imitate the answer to this question. Have fun! Kaitlyn and I had a lot of fun these many years of study. I understand more about the hopes and fears of her generation now, and she understands mine better also.

We will use the New American Standard Bible (NASB) for most biblical excerpts, but we strongly encourage you to have your Bible with you and to look up all verses for yourself.

INTRODUCTION

Have you ever felt alone? Fearful? Hopeless? Purposeless? Unsure of what to do? If you answered no to any of these questions, I must ask, are you even human? It is in our human nature to feel these anxieties and be discouraged sometimes.

It is in these times that people look for comfort and strength. The Holy Bible is filled with many great insights, encouragements, warnings, instructions, and parables, all of which by their very nature are a direct link to Yahweh (God) and His Son, Yeshua (Jesus).

In the New Testament book of John (10:1–30), there is a parable called the parable of the good shepherd where Yeshua (Jesus) demonstrates the relationship between Himself and His people. This story, like the Bible in general, gives us encouragement, instruction, and an idea of what the life of someone who follows Yeshua should look like.

Unlike a hired man who has no personal connection with a flock of sheep, Yeshua compares Himself to a good shepherd who is always ready to lay down His life for His sheep who know Him. In John 10:27–30 He says, "My sheep listen to My voice, and I know them, and they follow Me; and I give them eternal life, and they will never perish; and no one will snatch them out of My hand. My

Father, who has given them to Me, is greater than all; and no one is able to snatch them out of the Father's hand. I and the Father are one."

This reward of eternal life comes to those who know Him and seek a relationship with Him. But how can someone possibly know Him? What does their life look like? Do you know Him?

Daniel was one of the few people in the Bible who knew his God and followed Him wholeheartedly, never wavering, even amid persecution. He had resolved in his heart not to sway from God's instruction (Daniel 1:8). He knew the voice of the Lord and refused to follow the stranger who called out to him, even during the most uncertain times of his life. This act took great strength, which came from Daniel's knowledge and faith regarding the voice of his Good Shepherd.

"When he puts all his own sheep outside, he goes ahead of them, and the sheep follow him because they know his voice. However, a stranger they simply will not follow, but will flee from him, because they do not know the voice of strangers" (John 10:4–5).

Learning from Daniel's example allows us to deal with our own uncertain times, finding peace in the ultimate peace giver, companion, fear soother, purpose giver, and way maker—Yeshua.

Each and every one of us deals with uncertainty. I have eight wonderful grandchildren. I am concerned about the life they will live in this country and the uncertain world. I see a world filled with pain, frustration, and suffering. One of the most important roles we have on this earth is to teach our children, grandchildren, and those close to us biblical truths.

How do I help them through the uncertainty? How did Daniel

get through his circumstances? How did he become and stay close to the Lord, even in the midst of trials?

When I read the book of Daniel, I was amazed by the character of the young men around whom it is centered. The fact that their story unfolds during the absolute and utter destruction of their nation makes it even more impactful. How did they stand firm in their faith when they were just in their midteens?

What did their parents, and especially their grandparents, instill in them that enabled them to rise to the top and thrive there? Would my grandchildren, four of whom were fifteen when this book was started, be able to survive the pressures Daniel and his friends faced and prosper as they did?

I have studied the topic of Daniel and his strength for several years now, and I have only begun to understand the characteristics that gave him and his three friends their strength. My granddaughter, Kaitlyn, and I have identified key characteristics of Daniel and his three friends that we believe helped give them the strength they needed to stand firm in their faith despite the wickedness around them.

In this book we will discuss those characteristics, analyze parts of the book of Daniel, and learn how to teach that strength to the next generation as well as ourselves.

"What would happen if the people who see only the past and the people that see only the future were to turn around and face each other?"[1]

This question was asked by a woman named Barbara in the book *Heart of the Holy Land* by Paul Wright. Barbara was talking about the conflict in the Middle East, but the same question can be applied to our study of the book of Daniel and our relationships across generations. What would happen if generational barriers broke down and we turned to face each other?

What if old people (like me, a baby boomer) could break out of the mental rut of being stuck in the ways of the past and turn to the present generation with love?

What if Kaitlyn (Gen Z) could turn to people my age and ask for guidance and help in prayer, support, or wisdom?

What if I someday cheered Kaitlyn on when she gets the first job in her career field and has her first baby? What if Kaitlyn cheered me on when someday I make a complete circle around an assisted living facility using my walker without sitting down?

What if we faced each other with unconditional love and a desire to grow in Yeshua (Jesus) together? This was the approach we took while writing this study. We fully believe that communication and community are vital to maintain the strength needed to stay firm in our faith at any age.

That being said, my granddaughter and I want you to know, dear reader, that only one man on this earth, Yeshua, has ever had every answer to every question, can provide every comfort for every despair, and displays utter perfection despite the evil of this world.

It is to Yeshua we hope all readers of this book wish to draw near, and it is Him we hope we have pleased by studying the Word (the Bible) to learn about Daniel's strength. This book is about that kind of strength. We hope to apply the characteristics of Daniel and his friends to our own lives through a generational lens.

We hope you, dear reader, will have further insight into the lives and the strength of the four—Daniel (Belteshazzar), Hananiah

(Shadrach), Mishael (Meshach) and Azariah (Abed-nego)—and glean something to help one of our most precious gifts from God—the next generation.

ONE
VITAL INFORMATION

WHO IS DANIEL?

Linda

℮

While many of us have heard about Daniel in reference to the lions' den, there is so much more to Daniel's story than that.

Daniel was born in Jerusalem and raised with great accessibility to knowledge. He was well educated, probably had large portions of the Torah (the first five books of the Bible) memorized, and grew up in obedience to Yahweh (the name of God).

Daniel and his three friends were members of the nobility, so their families' status and wealth in the community gave them access to knowledge and a future in academics. Many other boys their age would have been doing manual labor.

Daniel and his friends were from the tribe of Judah, one of the twelve tribes of Israel, descended from Jacob, Isaac, and Abraham. These people lived in the southern kingdom of Israel.

Because of the tribe of Judah's disobedience to God, in 605 BC, when historians peg Daniel to have been in his midteens, the first wave of invasion into Judah by the Babylonians occurred. According to Flavius Josephus, a first-century scholar and author of the book *The Antiquities of the Jews*, King Nebuchadnezzar of Babylon, a Chaldean, kidnapped 10,832 young Hebrew men and women. Included in this number were members of the nobility, master craftsman, teachers, and priests. He brought them back to Babylon as a display of strength and pride. This group included Daniel and his three friends, Hananiah (Shadrach), Mishael (Meshach), and Azariah (Abed-nego).

They were forced into a life of servitude in the foreign, idol-worshipping world that was Babylon. In 586 BC Nebuchadnezzar came back to Jerusalem to finish the job. His soldiers came in and utterly destroyed the city, leaving nothing behind. The Babylonians pillaged and killed many, and the temple of God was annihilated and burned to the ground.

In Babylon these young captive Hebrews had their culture stripped from them and were forced to immerse themselves in a world that was completely foreign. There were new rules and customs that went against everything Daniel was used to and believed. Despite this lifestyle change, Daniel remained faithful to Yahweh (God) and strong in his obedience. Yahweh blessed him because of this faith and obedience.

Daniel and his friends' lives were spared by Yahweh on many occasions, and Daniel was granted wisdom that allowed him to rise through the ranks of the king of Babylon's advisors to become second in command.

Throughout his life, Daniel served the various kings of Babylon while staying utterly committed and devoted to God. Even when tested and tried, he never wavered in his faith and love for God, his country, Israel, and his family. Daniel became one of the greatest prophets ever to exist, and many of the revelations he was given by Yahweh are still being deciphered and studied today in preparation for times still to come.

We look to Daniel and the strength he displayed as an example of how to live our lives today. We will explore his attributes in greater detail in the following chapters.

EAST MEETS WEST

Linda

❡

Before Daniel's story can be further discussed, it is important to know the historical, cultural, and biblical significance behind the cities of Babylon and Jerusalem themselves.

East met West. Two cities collided. East conquered West and destroyed God's sanctuary (His temple) and the land. East killed most of the people who lived in the city. East took thousands of young people, priests, and prophets into slavery. East pillaged God's temple and carried away all the gold and silver as well as the golden Menorah.

East represents the city of Babylon, the city of Satan. West represents Jerusalem, the city of Yahweh. Jerusalem is also known as the city of peace, which means *shalom* in Hebrew. I find this name ironic as this city truly has yet to know peace. Only when Yeshua returns in the end of days will this city finally represent shalom.

In the future, God will reside in the holiest part of the temple, known as the mercy seat (the representation of the throne of God). Jerusalem is the city that Yeshua wept over (Matthew 23:37–39). The crucifixion occurred outside the gates of Jerusalem.

The city is first mentioned in Genesis 14:18. At that time, Melchizedek was the king of Salem (Jerusalem). He was priest of God Most High and blessed Abram. It is also the city of King David and King Solomon. Jerusalem is the city of all the kings and prophets in the Old Testament—it represents good, not evil.

Jerusalem was the epicenter of the world in ancient times, and in a spiritual way it still is today. The disciples were sent forth to evangelize the world from this city. The Word of God branched out from this city in the New Testament. Psalm 122:6 instructs us to pray for Jerusalem. It is the apple of God's eye (Zechariah 2:8). In the future the nations will be ruled from Zion (Jerusalem) and the law will go forth from there (Isaiah 2:3).

Today, Jerusalem is a city that is alive with people and tourists. It is the capital of Israel, and the United States embassy is now there. It has also been a city under siege at various points in Israel's existence from 1948 to present.

I have visited Jerusalem several times, and the greeting most spoken in passing is "Shalom, Shalom," meaning "Peace, Peace." But there is no peace because of the tensions between surrounding nations.

The city of Babylon, on the other hand, is the literary and physical representation of evil. This city was founded by Nimrod, as stated in the genealogy of Noah (Genesis 10). The name Nimrod in Hebrew means "to rebel," which is perfect for him. He was a mighty hunter before the Lord (Genesis 10:8–9).[1] Satan backed Nimrod in anger against God. Nimrod set up his government in ways that rebelled against the Lord.[2] His wife was Semiramis, who was also his mother.[3]

This satanic couple started the religion of the sun god, a religion practiced in Babylon as well as many other cultures of the world. While these cultures were polytheistic, meaning they worshipped many gods, they each had their own name for their sun god, or their primary god. To the Egyptians it was Ra, for the Greeks it was Zeus, to the Romans it was Mithra, and for the Babylonians it was Tammuz.[4]

The people of Babylon, referred to as "the children of men" in Genesis 11, were responsible for constructing one of the worst idols and affronts to God in human history, the Tower of Babel. God was displeased by this act and confused the language of the people who were building it.

As a result of God causing the people to be unable to understand one another's words, the Babylonians scattered across the land. This scattering spread their false religion to the ends of the earth, where it was adapted into the many forms we see today.

Semiramis also founded her own religion. Her name after death was Astarte, or Aphrodite to the Greeks. The Romans called her Venus, the Egyptians called her Isis, and the Canaanites called her Asherah or the Queen of Heaven. She gave birth to a son called Tammuz, who was killed by a wild boar at age forty.

Babylonians, and virtually all the scattered people from the Tower of Babel, had this religious system. There were festivals that included forty days of weeping for Tammuz every year to celebrate the forty years of his life. In Ezekiel 8:14 we see that this religion even entered the temple in Jerusalem. Virtually all occultic practices started in Babylon. The worship of the zodiac and horoscope are examples.

When Daniel and his three friends arrived in Babylon, they saw a city full of temples to many gods and a huge ziggurat, which was probably the actual remains of the Tower of Babel.

Babylon is mentioned in Revelation 18:10: "Woe, woe, the great city, Babylon, the strong city! For in one hour your judgment has come." Revelation 18:2 says Babylon "has become a dwelling place of demons and a prison of every unclean spirit, and a prison of every unclean and hateful bird." Her title is seen in Revelation 17:5: "BABYLON THE GREAT, THE MOTHER OF PROSTITUTES AND OF THE ABOMINATIONS OF THE EARTH."

Today, Babylon is in ruins; very few people live there. Saddam Hussein tried to resurrect it in 1983 but failed. He thought he was the reincarnation of ancient King Nebuchadnezzar.[5]

Two cities. Babylon and Jerusalem. East versus West. Good versus evil. The Lord says in His Word in Revelation 18:4 concerning Babylon, "Come out of her, my people, so that you will not participate in her sins and receive any of her plagues."

But Daniel and his three friends were kidnapped along with thousands of other young men and women, nobility, priests, and prophets, snatched from their homes in Jerusalem, to go East. In Psalm 137:1–6 we see the young men and women refusing to obey their captors on the way to Babylon:

> By the rivers of Babylon,
> There we sat down and wept,
> When we remembered Zion.
> Upon the willows in the midst of it

We hung our harps.
For there our captors demanded of us songs,
And our tormentors, jubilation, saying,
"Sing for us one of the songs of Zion!"

How can we sing the LORD's song
In a foreign land?
If I forget you, Jerusalem,
May my right hand forget its skill.
May my tongue cling to the roof of my mouth
If I do not remember you,
If I do not exalt Jerusalem
Above my chief joy.

Even though they were brought into Babylon, the city of sin, the Lord's will was still fulfilled through their story. As stated in Jeremiah 24:1–7, God was still with them in their captivity and blessed them.

THE CHARACTERISTICS OF DANIEL

Kaitlyn

Daniel and his friends were able to withstand the pressures and challenges of the corrupt world around them, which is why they are written about in such a positive light in the Bible. The Bible is the story of God's divine plan, playing out through His chosen people, where Yeshua plays a central role in the narrative. It is also a guidebook for how we should pursue God, worship Him, and live a life that glorifies Him. Because Daniel is written about in such a positive way, we will study some of the characteristics that led to his great strength and faith in order to take after his example. Each one of the characteristics listed below will be discussed in greater detail in the following chapters:

Daniel had strength.
Daniel had faith.
Daniel had obedience.
Daniel had devotion.
Daniel had knowledge.
Daniel had prayer.

CONNECTING THROUGH REFLECTIONS ON INTERGENERATIONAL COMMUNICATION

Kaitlyn

How would you define intergenerational communication? They are big words, they do *not* roll off the tongue easily, and, trust me, they were also a pain to type more than forty times throughout this book. Intergenerational communication is defined as "interactions between individuals from different age cohorts or age groups."[6] This foundation is vital to the concept of this book because conversing with individuals from different generations is fundamental to developing deeply meaningful relationships, particularly in the context of faith-based connection.

Intergenerational connections can occur in different facets of people's lives. Many rely on parents, close relatives, or friends to help decipher finances, give advice on raising children, and connect with God on a genuine level. Reflect on your own life. Do you have a similar relationship with someone? Are there times in your life when it feels like your spiritual strength has failed? Do you look to someone during these times? I guarantee that someone in your life has had similar thoughts or struggles. While we should always rely on Yahweh's Word and the Spirit who guides us, it is also important to join in community with those who have had similar experiences and can offer guidance.

There are many biblical examples of this concept: Paul and Timothy (1 Timothy 1:1–2), Naomi and Ruth (the book of Ruth), and Eli and Samuel (1 Samuel 3). In each of these pairs, people were able to share knowledge and experiences, care for and connect with each other, and share a mutual love for the heavenly Father. It is beneficial to communicate intergenerationally, particularly to the point of developing a personal and invested relationship, because of the gifts of knowledge, skill, and love that can be exchanged. These ideas are immensely valuable.

This does not mean, however, the path to intergenerational communication is an easy one. A downfall of the 150-character tweet culture that has developed in the last several years is the simplification and overgeneralization of entire generations. As funny as it is to laugh at an "okay, boomer" joke or a millennial's "participation trophy," we seem to have reinforced a barrier to real connection. Where the ideals of society prevail, it is easier to see roadblocks to connection rather than pathways to community. Humbling ourselves and working to search for pathways to community can be achieved through intergenerational communication. In this way, we too can experience relationships like Paul and Timothy, Naomi and Ruth, and Eli and Samuel.

How do we teach the strength of Daniel's character to the next generation and ourselves? The answer is simple: intergenerational connection through meaningful communication. This can be done by forming connections with others through an understanding of different contexts and backgrounds, joining in community through common action, building a foundation of love and acceptance, challenging each other to grow and learn, and investing in the futures of each other. This book demonstrates these elements of meaningful communication as they build off each other to create a deeper connection among people of different generations.

While there are many articles and studies that have been conducted to inform people about the dangers of a lack of intergenerational communication in the workforce, to our knowledge, these thoughts have not been applied to a religious setting except through the concept of mentorship.

Classic Christian mentorship is most commonly a relationship where the older guides the younger in the pursuit of Jesus. Our book seeks to build on the ideas of mentorship, but we do not wish to say that a mentorship relationship is the only place where intergenerational communication skills can be applied. As we utilize it, intergenerational communication exists within a connection where an interchanging flow of knowledge and perspectives occurs, where the younger can also teach the older. There are benefits to both kinds of relationships. In the process of writing we spoke with each other a lot about the similarities and subtle differences between the two applications of intergenerational communication. We debated how to capture the sentiment of interchangeability.

Ultimately, we also encourage intergenerational communication in an informal way. The ideas of communication presented in this book can be applied to decades-long relationships (like a mentorship) as surely as they can be applied to thirty-minute conversations with a random person you meet in a coffee shop. At the end of each chapter, there will be a section where we will expand on the characteristic of Daniel that was explored in that chapter (strength, faith, prayer, etc.), and build on the concept of fostering meaningful intergenerational connections.

TWO
DANIEL HAD STRENGTH

WHY DID JERUSALEM FALL?

Linda

W e know that Daniel was carted off to Babylon in 605 BC. But why did God allow him to be taken there? Why was Jerusalem destroyed? Daniel 1:1–2 says, "In the third year of the reign of Jehoiakim king of Judah, Nebuchadnezzar king of Babylon came to Jerusalem and besieged it. And the Lord handed Jehoiakim king of Judah over to him, along with some of the vessels of the house of God; and he brought them to the land of Shinar, to the house of his god, and he brought the vessels into the treasury of his god."

To understand this era, and why the Elohim of Abraham, Isaac, and Jacob allowed destruction to befall His chosen people, let's turn to the Word.

Read Ezekiel 8. Ezekiel was a prophet of God Most High who lived around the same time as Daniel. What did he see? God caught Ezekiel by the lock of his head and took him to Jerusalem, specifically to the temple of God. God showed him the disobedience of the people of Israel.

The Israelites' actions were wrong because God had set the people of Israel apart to worship only Him in *His* way, not in the way of man. What specific abominations did Ezekiel see inside this place of worship?

- The idol of jealousy, the Asherah, was at the entrance to the north gate of the inner court (Ezekiel 8:3).

- Ezekiel dug a hole inside the temple and discovered every form of creeping thing. Beasts and idols were carved on the wall. This was the animal worship of the Egyptian cult inside the temple itself (Ezekiel 8:8–10).

- The seventy elders of Israel were seen with incense used to worship other gods in the heart of Yahweh's temple (Ezekiel 8:11).

- Women were weeping for Tammuz, a Babylonian god that demanded the sacrifice of children (Ezekiel 8:14).

- In the sacred inner court, twenty-five men, with their backs to the temple, were worshipping the sun as an idol. These twenty-five men represented the twenty-four orders of the priests plus the high priest (Ezekiel 8:16).[1]

- "Putting the twig to their nose" refers to nature worship. This was also done inside the temple (Ezekiel 8:17).

All this was happening inside the temple! In the very place where God was to reside in the holy of holies, between the cherubim on the mercy seat of the ark of the covenant, the people were unabashedly worshipping other gods. Priests, elders, and women were doing these evil things in God's temple. This was *not* what they were called to do. They messed up big time.

Let's take a look at Jeremiah, who was a major prophet at the time of Daniel and Ezekiel. In Jeremiah 7:17–18 he writes, "Do you not see what they are doing in the cities of Judah and in the streets of Jerusalem? The children gather wood, the fathers kindle the fire, and the women knead dough to make sacrificial cakes for the queen of heaven; and they pour out drink offerings to other gods in order to provoke Me to anger."

In Jerusalem, the children gathered the wood, the father kindled the fire, and the women made cakes to the Queen of Heaven (also known as Semiramis) and made offerings to other gods and goddesses to spite Yahweh. Idolatry was a family affair!

The Queen of Heaven was a goddess in the Babylonian belief system who routinely practiced infant killings and sacrifice. The people in Jerusalem were not doing the things they were supposed to, and they were destroying the sacredness of Elohim and his temple.

What did God have to say to them? Keep reading in Jeremiah 7:19–20, "'Are they provoking Me?' declares the LORD. 'Is it not themselves instead, to their own shame?' Therefore this is what the Lord GOD says, 'Behold, My anger and My wrath will be poured out on this place, on human and animal life, and on the trees of the field and the fruit of the ground; and it will burn and not be quenched.'"

God planned to right the wrongs the people had committed and allowed them to be destroyed and taken to Babylon. Being a merciful God, He did give Jerusalem the opportunity to avoid death and destruction if they would allow themselves to be taken away peacefully. The prophet Jeremiah was tasked with giving this word from God to the King of Israel, Zedekiah (Jeremiah 21:8–10).

King Zedekiah did not heed this advice. He believed that the walls around Jerusalem would save them from their destruction. The nation waited in the city, falsely thinking they could save themselves and destroy the armies of Babylon without the help of God. This did not go well for them.

According to Josephus, a first-century Jew who wrote the most complete surviving history of the Jewish people and Romans from creation through the reign of Nero, Babylon's army painstakingly built great walls of dirt around the city (which can still be seen today, more than twenty-five hundred years later) that barricaded the Israelites in, and eventually forced them out easily. Prophet after prophet of Elohim, including the likes of Jeremiah, Habakkuk, Micah, and Ezekiel, tried warning the nation. But those inside the wall just sat in their homes, watched, and waited. Yikes!

HOW DID JERUSALEM FALL?

Linda

◯

S
o far, we have seen how the destruction of Jerusalem was prophesied to occur, but what did that destruction actually look like? We have already discussed how Babylon came in and built huge berms around the city walls that they used to imprison the people inside. They also used these berms to fire arrows at the people.

For eighteen months the people of the city were subjected to a lack of food and famine because of their imprisonment. In Habakkuk 3:17–18 the prophet Habakkuk describes the condition of the land because of the berms and imprisonment: "Even if the fig tree does not blossom, and there is no fruit on the vines, if the yield of the olive fails, and the fields produce no food, even if the flock disappears from the fold, and there be no cattle in the stalls, yet I will triumph in the LORD, I will rejoice in the God of my salvation."

Fig trees take five or six years to bloom, and grape vines require seven years before grapes are ripe. The olive tree takes five to twenty years before its fruit can be harvested, depending on its type. If these types of vegetation are destroyed, it takes years to recover what was lost.

This verse also says that the fields were barren and the sheep and cows were gone. So where did all this food go? The Babylonians ate it! Habakkuk sees the Babylonians circling and setting up to destroy them. There are many of them. Hundreds of thousands of gifted men of war equipped with armor and shields were ready and hungry for battle.[2]

All of these men descended on the fields surrounding the city and were supported by the existing food source. This meant that the inhabitants of the city were forced into starvation and became weaker and weaker.[3]

The eighteen-month siege was horrific.[4] When the Babylonian army finally besieged the city, the inhabitants of Jerusalem were too weak to fight and immediately surrendered to them. Women and children were raped and killed, people were beheaded, pregnant women had their infants cut out of them.

Mayhem after mayhem, the temple was burned and destroyed. Anarchy, helplessness, and hopelessness were everywhere. Everything they cherished was lost. Normal was annihilated. Their future—gone. It is hard even to imagine the scene of despair.

Those who survived the destruction were the nobility children. These children showed intellectual promise, and they were probably young and attractive. Daniel, his three friends, and others were taken before their homeland was eventually destroyed.

Read Daniel 1:1–4:

> In the third year of the reign of Jehoiakim king
> of Judah, Nebuchadnezzar king of Babylon
> came to Jerusalem and besieged it. And the Lord
> handed Jehoiakim king of Judah over to him,
> along with some of the vessels of the house of
> God; and he brought them to the land of Shinar,
> to the house of his god, and he brought the
> vessels into the treasury of his god.
>
> Then the king ordered Ashpenaz, the chief of
> his officials, to bring in some of the sons of
> Israel, including some of the royal family and
> of the nobles, youths in whom there was no
> impairment, who were good-looking, suitable for
> instruction in every kind of expertise, endowed
> with understanding and discerning knowledge,
> and who had ability to serve in the king's court;
> and he ordered Ashpenaz to teach them the
> literature and language of the Chaldeans.

This is how Daniel and his three friends were taken to the land of Shinar (Babylon) with treasured items, which they likely carried by hand. Throughout Daniel chapter 1, it becomes clear that God was angry. The Bible describes the destruction in Jerusalem that caused these young men to be taken away as both prophesied and warranted because of the people's disobedience and hardened hearts.

Through this destruction of Daniel's life, family, and homeland, do we see a young man in despair? Or do we see a young man who is still following God's Torah and praising, praying, and worshipping the God of the universe?

What we see in this book is a young man who is strong. Not just through the physical test of strength by being kidnapped and taken into a life of servitude, but also mentally and spiritually as he maintained his culture and devotion to God. He is strong in his faith and love for Yahweh. We see a young man grounded in the Word. The knowledge he received, passed down from generation to generation, holds him through his long life in exile.

CONNECTING THROUGH REFLECTIONS ON STRENGTH

Kaitlyn

❧

Think of times when it felt as if your whole world was destroyed like Daniel's, when none of your plans went how you wanted. When control of your day, life, and emotions seemed hard to grasp. Were there times when God seemed intangible, too quiet, or just too far away? These are times when we feel weak. The time during which Daniel and others were taken represented an all-time low in Israel's history. It was a time of vulnerability, sorrow, and weakness. For Daniel and his friends, God surely must have felt far away, as He does at times for us.

Daniel is an example for us during times of weakness. In this chapter we have seen how his circumstances consisted of unique hardships. Elohim directed him to submit to the Babylonian king's rule, in a nation of sin, amid the destruction of the secure future in Jerusalem that he had anticipated. His strength was proven by his survival of the many horrible situations he was put through. Daniel found strength in God's Word and his relationship with God. Daniel teaches us that strength can come during times of weakness and vulnerability.

His journey is likely very different from ours, but just as we strive to understand Daniel's strength, we must strive to learn about the context of each other's strength, which can be done through intergenerational communication.

Each person has a unique story because of their culture and background. A first step to intergenerational communication is recognizing that there are differences in every person, and it's important to inquire about those differences. Anyone can start the conversation—maybe it is the older person, maybe it is the younger. The goal is to share experiences. This may be as simple as small talk or getting to know someone for the first time. How old are they? Where are they from? Do they have siblings? What is their career? Did they go to college? What did they enjoy studying in school? Are they married? Do they have any pets? This list can go on and on and should be tailored to each conversation.

Every person is a child of God and unique in their own way. Recognizing differences in each person's background, and joining in community through the inevitable similarities that we do have, allows us to share our strengths with each other. The simple (and yet not so simple) act of respectfully sharing experiences, beliefs, and ideas must start with a willingness to understand that each person is unique in their strength. The process of sharing contexts ultimately forms connections with each other that is built by meaningful intergenerational communication.

THREE
DANIEL HAD FAITH

AN EXAMPLE OF FAITH

Linda

Daniel was a teenager when he was taken to Babylon, and he was in his eighties when he received his last vision. Through those years his faith in God never wavered (as recorded by the Word). It would have been extremely difficult to continually praise, worship, and trust in his heavenly Father when everyone in sight was worshipping idols.

When the very air they breathed was against Elohim, how did the four survive alone without the family and friends who had surrounded them back in Jerusalem? They were praising their heavenly Father three times a day on their knees, giving thanks and interceding on behalf of the nation of Israel (Daniel 6:10). They did not give in to the pressures of Babylon that they faced year after year after year.

The story found in Daniel 6 perfectly showcases Daniel's faith. This chapter is probably one of the most loved chapters in the Bible; virtually every child who has gone to Sunday school knows about Daniel and the lions' den. Read Daniel 6 carefully.

In this chapter, Daniel was placed in charge of 120 princes. The 120 princes decided to undermine Daniel's authority, but they could find no fault in him. How can you destroy someone who appears to be perfect? They wondered if he had any weakness at all.

The 120 decided Daniel's weakness was his faith in the one true God. They did not like the fact that Daniel held his God above the king and thought they could exploit him in this way. They appealed to Darius's pride by proclaiming that he and only he was worthy of worship, and the king fell for it. Darius's pride and self-importance almost cost Daniel his life.

To paraphrase, the leaders said to King Darius, "Did you not give a decree that for one month only you are to be worshipped? Well, Daniel has not followed your law. You are the absolute authority of the Meads and Persians, yet he is worshipping his God three times a day."

After Daniel was arrested, Darius became mad at himself for falling for this trick. He was also mad at Daniel. He probably thought, *Couldn't you just take one month off?* He likely was mad at Daniel's God too: *Why does he require so much dedication and worship?*

Was Daniel afraid when he was dropped in the lions' pit? I would be. Did he remember the stories that his three friends told him about the fiery furnace? (See Daniel 3.) Did his faith waver, or did he say to himself, *No matter what happens I will praise Elohim?* Daniel spent a night with the lions.

All the Bible depictions you see of this event show Daniel sitting with the lions roaming around him. Was he sitting or standing? Was he hiding in a corner? Was he praying? Did he spend this night on his knees, praising and giving thanks? The Bible doesn't say.

The next day dawned, and King Darius (after a fitful, sleepless night of worry for his friend) ran to the pit. "And when he had come near the den to Daniel, he cried out with a troubled voice. The king began speaking and said to Daniel, 'Daniel, servant of the living God, has your God, whom you continually serve, been able to rescue you from the lions?' Then Daniel spoke to the king, "O king, live forever! My God sent His angel and shut the lions' mouths, and they have not harmed me, since I was found innocent before Him; and also toward you, O king, I have committed no crime'" (Daniel 6:20–22).

The king was exceedingly glad that God had saved Daniel. When Darius's servants pulled him from the pit, not a scratch was found on Daniel. In Daniel chapter 6 we see several verses that display Daniel's faith in God:

- Three times a day he prayed and gave thanks (v. 10).
- Daniel served God continuously (v. 16).
- He was innocent (v. 22).
- He believed in God (v. 23).

Throughout the entire Word of God (Old Testament and New Testament), we have examples of incredible faith. What is the definition of faith? According to Hebrews 11:1, "faith is the certainty of things hoped for, a proof of things not seen." Faith means trust; faith means that you turn everything—every worry, every frustration, every pain, every concern, and even every joy . . . *everything*—over to the sovereign God of the universe.

See Hebrews 11. Abel, Enoch, Noah, Abraham, Sarah, Isaac, Jacob, Joseph, Moses, Rahab, Gideon, Barak, Samson, Jephthah, David, Samuel, and the prophets . . . all of these Old Testament people exhibited faith. The New Testament also has many examples of people with enormous faith. All the disciples had faith; the first martyr, Stephen, had it, as well as Paul, Timothy, Aquilla and Priscila, Lydia, James, and the list goes on and on.

But where did this faith come from? Did it just drop out of the sky? Look up Romans 10:17 (KJV): "So then faith cometh by hearing, and hearing by the word of God." When we look at Daniel and his three friends, where did they first hear the Word of God? At home.

Daniel and his three friends began their education learning the Torah (the first five books of the Bible) in the Tanakh (the Old Testament). The book *See Spot Run!* with Dick and Jane would not have been part of their curriculum. By the time these young men were beginning their adult relationships with God at the age of thirteen, they would have put all or most of the Torah to memory.

But just because they grew up learning about the Word doesn't mean their faith was automatically ingrained. They had to choose continually to develop their relationship with God. In the same way, someone who has not grown up learning about God can choose to develop their relationship with Him at any time.

That said, their strong faith came from *hearing* and *knowing* the Word of God. This is one of the ways, according to Paul in Romans

10:17, that God helps us have faith in Him. This does not mean the process is an easy one. This does not mean that faith comes easy. Faith is alive; it must be fed, watered, and nurtured to grow. Hearing a pastor or teacher comment on the Word is a great way to supplement one's knowledge of a biblical subject. Ultimately, however, biblical faith comes from God through our studying and hearing His Word, Genesis through Revelation. Read it out loud to yourself, and delight in the truth of His Word, for that is how Daniel and his three friends developed the active faith that sustained them through their captivity.

A FOUNDATION OF FAITH AND TRUST IN OUR HEAVENLY FATHER

Linda

P salm 71:17–18 says, "God, You have taught me from my youth, and I still declare Your wondrous deeds. And even when I am old and gray, God, do not abandon me, until I declare Your strength to this generation, Your power to all who are to come."

As a grandmother of eight very different and wonderful grandchildren, I meditate on this verse as I plead with the Father that I can maintain strength in my old age and gray hair to witness to the generation of my grandchildren. To every grandparent who is reading this, the goal of your life should be to grow the spiritual health of the next generations. Do not focus on a material legacy but leave them with the eternal blessing of knowing their heavenly Father.

Ask the Lord to reveal Himself to you. As Jeremiah 29:11–13 says, "'For I know the plans that I have for you,' declares the LORD, 'plans for prosperity and not for disaster, to give you a future and a hope. Then you will call upon Me and come and pray to Me, and

I will listen to you. And you will seek Me and find Me when you search for Me with all your heart.'"

Are you searching for God? The promise to find Him is in verse 13: "You will seek Me and find Me when you search for Me with all your heart." Seeking Him involves having faith and walking in the right direction until you see the Light that is Yeshua. When the future seems uncertain and we feel as if we are walking blind, it takes acceptance of that blindness to trust in God and follow the light of Yeshua. I have to trust that God will provide and lead me in the right direction if I strive for it.

Thinking about this concept reminds me of a story my dad once told me. My dad, Leonard, lived to be eighty-nine years old and golfed up until the very day he had a stroke that ended his life. He had played golf for almost seventy years. He once told me a story of one of his golfing adventures in Arizona many years ago. The golf course is called Painted Mountain and is still beautiful today. It is located in the desert of Arizona with the beauty of God's creation all around.

My dad and a friend started walking this majestic course from hole to hole until they reached the ninth hole, miles from the clubhouse. Concentrating only on their next shot, they lost track of the time and what little daylight they had left.

The sun went behind those God-painted mountains, and darkness descended on them in a heartbeat. This was a darkness you could almost feel, and they could not see their hands in front of their faces. Darkness in the desert, even on a golf course, is frightening.

Many of God's creatures, like coyotes, snakes, scorpions, and jumping spiders, to name a few, come out at night. They were both really scared. They started walking very carefully in the direction they thought the clubhouse might be, and when they saw a distant light, they walked toward it to safety.

Are you lost? Are you afraid? Are you surrounded by evil and things that want to harm you? When we experience times of stress and anxiety, it is important to remember to take a step back and realize that we are walking in the dark. Even in the dark, do we realize that Yeshua is with us? He is here holding our hand and walking ahead of us. When you see the Light, walk toward that Light—it is the Messiah. "Your word is a lamp to my feet and a light to my path" (Psalm 119:105). Trust that God will lead you, one way or another.

Continually searching for Yahweh is the way to find and maintain a faith-filled foundational relationship. This is the same kind of searching and foundation building that Daniel did. Daniel had a great foundation that helped keep him strong. What is your foundation?

CONNECTING THROUGH REFLECTIONS ON FAITH

Kaitlyn

❧

Daniel was taken from a place of spiritual light to a place of spiritual darkness, but in the darkness of his new surroundings, he relied on the light from the faith he grew up with. This was his journey; what is yours? How new or old is your faith? What roadblocks have you come up against?

After you have humbled yourself to know that the person you are having an intergenerational conversation with has a different context than you, it is easier to recognize that they also have a different experience with faith. We can build meaningful intergenerational communication by moving past the small talk that helps us understand each other's context and into more difficult conversations about how each person experiences God. This is where the faith of the other person becomes the center of the conversation.

What can I share with my grandmother about faith that would be new to her? The answer may be easier in the reverse, which is why mentorship relationships rely on the passing of knowledge and wisdom. However, in an intergenerational approach there is always something to learn from another. It is important to have an intergenerational conversation about faith because each person, each generation, brings something different to the table because of their background and perspectives.

Comparatively, a young person's faith is probably more centered on hope and expectations for the future. They may need and have more faith that God *will* provide a great career or family, He *will* guide them through choices, He *will* accompany them in sorrow, and He *will* be faithful.

An older person's faith may be more centered on the knowledge that God did provide. God *did* provide a career or family, He *did* guide them through choices, He *did* accompany them in sorrow, and He *was* faithful. An older person may realize that God *was* with them and He *will* continue to be with them, their children, their grandchildren, their great grandchildren, and so on.

These perspectives are different enough that conversations with each other may prompt great discussions about faith. Faith is a personal thing. Though it is experienced differently for each person, each person has been given a measure of faith (Romans 12:3). This means that everyone has some experience to share—so share it.

Throughout college I had the privilege of meeting amazing people who pushed me spiritually. It was uncomfortable for me to share my faith, even in private conversations with friends. But because of these moments, my experience with faith has changed for the better. Because of strong peers and mentors, in addition to the time I've spent with my grandma, I have been pushed to experience faith differently than I ever have before.

In intergenerational conversations, we must brave the discomfort that comes with sharing our experiences to trust that God is with us and that the other person is willing to listen to what we have to say, just as we are ready to listen to them.

Even though Yahweh is our most important common ground, an intergenerational conversation does not need to start with the sharing of deeply personal faith experiences. That is where the building of context comes in—it may start with a common love of puppies (this would be me!) or a baseball team (this would not be me). That said, it is so important to share personal experiences in order to gain commonality and build a foundation of trust in each other that can carry into a deeper study of our heavenly Father.

FOUR
DANIEL HAD OBEDIENCE

DANIEL'S OBEDIENCE: AN ACT OF FAITH AND LOVE

Kaitlyn

Perhaps one of Daniel's most difficult characteristics for us to understand and apply to our lives is that of obedience. It can be called "difficult" because of the intricacy and misinterpretation of what obedience is and how important it is in our lives today.

In previous chapters we discussed the concept of Daniel's faith. Faith can primarily be defined by Hebrews 11:1: "Now faith is the certainty of things hoped for, a proof of things not seen." Daniel, like many other biblical figures, was the embodiment of this definition and exhibited the faith that Hebrews 11 goes on to discuss.

Read all of Hebrews 11 carefully. This chapter lays out the importance of actions that come from obedience because of faith.

The literary parallel in each verse shows that by *faith* someone had the capacity to *obey* Yahweh and listen to His voice amid their uncertainty. This chapter is fascinating because it reveals the importance of the next step after having faith. It was not enough for the biblical heroes of Hebrews 11 to believe that Yahweh existed. Yahweh expected them to *show* their faith and take the next step by obeying what He told them to do. This obedience is a form of love for Him.

Let's single out Hebrews 11:7 as an example. "By faith Noah, being warned by God about things not yet seen, in reverence prepared an ark for the salvation of his household, by which he condemned the world, and became an heir of the righteousness which is according to faith."

Noah was described as a righteous man, a man who did what was pleasing in the eyes of Elohim. That being said, when Noah was called by God to make a huge boat to carry the only remnants of life to safety when a massive flood came to annihilate the rest of the earth, he probably got a few looks. Still, Noah obeyed the voice of God and built the ark.

Faith is intricately linked to obedience. But what is obedience? Why is it important? How did Daniel show this trait? Should today's believers be obedient?

Obedience is a common theme throughout the biblical narrative. From beginning to end, obedience is emphasized by Moses, the prophets, Paul, James, and especially Yeshua. The giving of the Law through Moses may have been the first official written record of the expectations God has for His people, but an oral passing down of rules to obey has existed since the garden of Eden.

Things went well for God's people (Israel) when they followed these commands, and things did not go well when they didn't (Deuteronomy 27:9–28:68). Look no further than the destruction of Jerusalem, as discussed in this book, to see that.

The faithless, disobedient actions of the people of Judah (referring to both the tribe and the land that included Jerusalem) caused them to be wiped out. They went through a long period of "going through the motions" where they may have thought they were being obedient to God's commands, but they really were not. For example, they performed the sacrifices Yahweh called for, but they did not have the right intention behind them, which is evident by their mixing of practices in Yahweh's temple (Ezekiel 8).

The people probably thought they could do their own thing and God would be okay with it because His name was still involved. We know this is *not* the case. It is even forbidden in the Ten Commandments: "You shall not make for yourself an idol, or any likeness of what is in heaven above or on the earth beneath, or in the water under the earth. You shall not worship them nor serve them; for I, the LORD your God, am a jealous God, inflicting the punishment of the fathers on the children, on the third and the fourth generations of those who hate Me, but showing favor to thousands, to those who love Me and keep My commandments" (Exodus 20:4–6).

It is important to remember that Elohim views a mixing of practices to be just as, if not more, abhorrent than worshipping other gods outright (see Ezekiel 8).

Clearly, God's people went through periods where they were not as obedient as they should have been. What set Daniel and his three friends apart from those around them? Their faith, which was displayed by their *obedience*.

How can we avoid merely going through the motions? Why should we be obedient to God as Daniel was? God wants a relationship with us, which develops by being obedient to His Word.

Daniel obeyed God by being dedicated to his heritage, by being faithful to God's commands in the Torah, by being steadfast through challenges, and by acting according to God's will. He learned God's will by prioritizing Yahweh over himself. Setting himself apart grew his wisdom, because he valued what was right by divine standards (God's standards), not by worldly standards.

Obedience requires sacrifice. According to worldly standards, it often doesn't make sense. In this way it realigns our priorities and humbles us. It challenges us. We have to trust that God loves us—a fact made abundantly clear in Scripture.

Logically, many of Daniel's choices don't make sense. In retrospect we can see how his decisions were beneficial for both him and the people he influenced, but at the time he was just obeying the God he loved. There likely was no thought that his story would be read and analyzed twenty-five hundred years later.

The same can be said for his three friends. When they walked into the fiery furnace, they likely did not think they would survive, let alone have their stories recorded in the Bible.

These young men knew how to listen to God's will in their lives. They were directed by His Word. They were directed by the Torah.

Why should someone be obedient to God via the Torah? An answer to this is found in John 14:23–24: "Jesus answered and said to him, 'If anyone loves Me, he will follow My word; and My Father will love him, and We will come to him and make Our dwelling with him. The one who does not love Me does not follow My words; and the word which you hear is not Mine, but the Father's who sent Me.'"

Obedience is associated with submission; submission is a form of humility and respect. God sees obedience as a form of love. God showed us how to live—He gave us direction in the Word and through the Holy Spirit who lives within us. This is seen in John 14:25–26: "These things I have spoken to you while remaining with you. But the Helper, the Holy Spirit whom the Father will send in My name, He will teach you all things, and remind you of all that I said to you."

Daniel was repeatedly humbled throughout his life. He went from noble to slave, from official to prisoner, from friend to condemned. This humbling allowed him to realize that he was not in control; his life was not his own.

Daniel knew he was a child of God, but his lifetime was nothing more than a wisp of the wind. A moment in an eternity. Yet God's love for Daniel gave his life meaning and value. If we refuse to reciprocate that love, as shown through our obedience, we reject the purpose God gives us. If Daniel had rejected the Torah and conformed to the Babylonian expectations, he would not have found favor in God. He would not have found his purpose *in* the ultimate purpose giver. God gives our lives meaning and value; we need to reach out to our heavenly Father and obey His words.

The practices that God wanted Daniel to participate in were very different from the Babylonian culture at that time. He was required to be set apart from the pagan practices for many reasons. This is a big deal. It would have been relatively easy to assimilate into the Babylonian culture. But he resisted the assimilation so that he could exhibit his obedience to God.

At the end of the day there is not enough space in this book, nor do I feel like I have the wisdom, to discuss all the concepts of obedience in depth. However, I will say that the only book one *must* read to understand the specific concepts involved in obedience is the Bible itself. *All* aspects of obedience we have discussed in this book are supported and commanded biblically.

After all I have learned about biblical love and its connection to obedience, I choose to be intentional about following the path of life laid out in the Bible.

OBEDIENCE UNDER FIRE — THE WEEPING PROPHET

Linda

℮

While Daniel and his three friends were kidnapped from their homes and walked to a pagan idol-worshipping country, while the four refused to eat the king's food, and while the fiery furnace was heating up, we have Elohim, King of the universe, approaching another young man in the land of Benjamin. His name was Jeremiah.

Jeremiah was the son of a priest (Jeremiah 1:1) who grew up with the knowledge of God. He was called into the service of Yahweh. In his own words, "Now the word of the LORD came to me, saying, 'Before I formed you in the womb I knew you, and before you were born I consecrated you; I have appointed you as a prophet to the nations'" (Jeremiah 1:4–5).

Was Jeremiah excited to be called into service as a prophet? Not at all. In fact, his first response to Yahweh Himself was no. He did not believe he could be of service at that time in his life because he was a youth.

The term *youth* in the Old Testament refers to someone younger than age twenty. When a person turned twenty, they were societally considered an adult. Twenty is the age of accountability in Scripture, and it's at that time a boy is called a man (Exodus 38:26). Twenty is also the age a man is eligible to go to war (Numbers 1:3).

Jeremiah was a youth around the same age as Daniel and his three friends when they were called to be witnesses to Babylon and Jerusalem.

Yahweh told Jeremiah, "Do not say, 'I am a youth,' because everywhere I send you, you shall go, and all that I command you, you shall speak. Do not be afraid of them, for I am with you to save you" (Jeremiah 1:7–8).

Through this verse, I want to show my grandchildren that God is with them. Do not be afraid, and do not be limited by your youth. God used young people like Jeremiah, Daniel, Hananiah, Mishael, Azariah, and others throughout the Bible to fulfill His plan. It is encouraging to know that Yahweh is there to save us, so we need not be afraid. He says to us, "Have I not commanded you? Be strong and courageous! Do not be terrified nor dismayed, for the LORD your God is with you wherever you go" (Joshua 1:9).

Jeremiah goes on to describe the way in which God was with him: "Then the LORD stretched out His hand and touched my mouth, and the LORD said to me, 'Behold, I have put My words in your mouth. See, I have appointed you this day over the nations and over the kingdoms, to root out and to tear down, to destroy and to overthrow, to build and to plant'" (Jeremiah 1:9–10).

In this young man we see a very reluctant prophet. He had weighed the cost of following the Lord; the burden of this decision would have almost been unbearable.

The Lord "gave words" to Jeremiah's mouth, as verse nine is directly translated from Hebrew, and Jeremiah was made a watchman for the nation and God's chosen people. He was to proclaim prophecy after prophecy of death, destruction, annihilation, pestilence, and famine. Jerusalem and its temple were going to be destroyed. People came to hate Jeremiah, and there were those who wanted to kill him because of his prophecies.

People would see him coming and run the other way. There were false prophets who would contradict every word from Jeremiah, and the people would accept every word the false prophets said. The people would ignore Jeremiah's words, or worse. According to Josephus as well as Jeremiah 38:6–12, Jeremiah was kidnapped and put into a cistern until he was up to his chin in mud. How did Jeremiah get out of this mire? Read Jeremiah 38:11–13 to find the answer.

As far as I can tell, not one person throughout his whole ministry believed him until His words (Yahweh's words) came true. But by that time, it was too late to save the people of Jerusalem.

Jeremiah was a reluctant prophet, famously known as the weeping prophet. He spent his whole life in a depressive state (Jeremiah 4:19; 10:19–20). He had no friends, no family, no wife, and was tormented every day. Jeremiah 12:6 states that even his brothers and the household of his father had dealt treacherously with him. He prophesized terrible things, then saw them fulfilled with his own eyes.

Jeremiah was called by the Lord at a young age, and his whole life was changed. It was not a pleasant or happy life. He is not an example of an individual living the "prosperity gospel" we can hear every day in some churches and on TV. Jeremiah is an example of someone who went through real-life struggles. He is an example of someone who took up his cross to follow Yeshua daily. He gave up *everything* to obey God.

Why? Why choose to be a Jeremiah? Or a Daniel, Hananiah, Mishael, or Azariah? Throughout this book we have placed ourselves in their shoes to visualize the physical struggles they went through daily—we know it was not a pretty picture. Time and time again we have seen the battles, destruction, loneliness, self-sacrifice, and idol-worshipping that filled their lives. Why would someone commit to God like Jeremiah or Daniel and his friends did?

Kaitlyn and I have discussed this ad nauseam. The truth is, not everyone does. There is a reason these five young men are written about in the Bible and their stories have been told for thousands of years. That being said, all of us will have situations in our lives that are intense, where we must make decisions for the greater good that will impact us and the world around us.

We can still learn from the lives of Jeremiah, Daniel, Hananiah, Mishael, and Azariah. We can learn how they handled their struggles and apply their characteristics to our lives. We can be encouraged by their strength. We have the same powerful God who carried them in their struggles. Remember what God has said: "Have I not commanded you? Be strong and courageous! Do not be terrified nor dismayed, for the LORD your God is with you wherever you go" (Joshua 1:9).

Why should you choose to obey Elohim? Why should you hope or have faith? Why study and seek His face? Do you think Jeremiah or Daniel asked that question a thousand or ten thousand times? What kept them going in times of trial, persecution, and pain?

I picture Jeremiah in the cistern with mud almost up to his eyeballs, looking up to heaven and saying, "Really, Lord? Is this necessary?"

Are you, dear reader, looking up and saying, "Really, why?" Throughout this book we have emphasized the concept of struggle and shown how hard the lives of Jeremiah, Daniel, and his three friends were. But isn't it true that our lives today are just as filled with struggle? Sometimes it feels impossible to get past the wrongs in this world.

However, Jeremiah had faith, love, and trust in his heavenly Father even in the midst of absolute turmoil. We are studying his life now, twenty-five hundred years later, and yet we are still encouraged by his perseverance.

Do you think Jeremiah, who is undoubtedly in heaven, would choose to do his life over again with the same struggles? Was it worth it, Jeremiah?

"Oh yeah. It was worth it."

I imagine this being his response. I can see Jeremiah looking down on us from heaven and saying, "Look, Father, I encouraged them by my life."

And the Father saying to him, "My good and faithful servant, come and see what I have prepared for you for eternity."

CONNECTING THROUGH REFLECTIONS ON OBEDIENCE

Kaitlyn

◟

Do you ever wish you were a dog? I know it sounds strange, but sometimes I envy the life of my dog, Daisy. Now, I know she is not the average dog—she is in the top 1 percent of puppies, living the life as the sole benefactor of a DINKWAD family (Double Income No Kids with a Dog)—but she seems to have a relatively simple life.

She never worries about her next meal, she has so many toys to de-stuff, she is always able to find a warm place to sleep in one of the five "beds" we have set up for her around the house, she has the sole attention of her two humans who pet and cuddle her before bed every night, she is social and gets to play with her puppy friends across town at least a couple of times a week, and she spends most of her day on the back of a couch looking out the massive window to watch cars and people (and probably many squirrels) pass by. She is soft, she is energetic, she is smart, she is silly, she is protective, and most important, she is so filled with love that pours out on all those around her. Why can't I be Daisy?

Like many in my generation, I have been through more changes in the past month, let alone the past five years, than Daisy will likely see in her lifetime. And a recent test that my husband and I took to measure our stress levels based on stressful life events found me at almost double the threshold for "major" stress—I was off the charts. This is a fact that is easier to laugh off than to deal with sometimes. It is hard to listen and obey the voice of God when stress is overwhelming.

There are many stressors in my life: Where will my husband get a job? Will we be able to find affordable housing nearby that will also accept Daisy? Will the housing be close enough to commute to my work and our family? When will we be able to start paying off our debt? How many years will it take until I feel settled? Through all of this I am often left confused, worried, and overwhelmed with the stress of being an overpreparer unable to prepare.

But, I am a child of the ultimate planner, and He is not confused by my path. He is not confused by your future, dear reader. He has a plan. I encourage you to remind yourself of this promise often and meditate on the words He has given us when we feel confused with where His voice is calling us.

"Many are the plans in a person's heart, but it is the Lord's purpose that prevails."
(Proverbs 19:21 NIV)

"'For I know the plans I have for you,' declares the
Lord, 'plans to prosper you and not to harm you,
plans to give you hope and a future.'"
(Jeremiah 29:11 NIV)

"Take delight in the Lord, and he will give you the
desires of your heart. Commit your way to the Lord;
trust in him and he will do this."
(Psalm 37:4–5 NIV)

"I will instruct you and teach you in the way you
should go; I will counsel you with my
loving eye on you."
(Psalm 32:8 NIV)

"Trust in the Lord with all your heart and lean not
on your own understanding; in all your ways submit
to him, and he will make your paths straight."
(Proverbs 3:5–6 NIV)

"You will keep in perfect peace those whose minds
are steadfast, because they trust in you."
(Isaiah 26:3 NIV)

Daniel was an excellent listener. Even without a burning bush
or a whisper in the wind as other prophets had received, Daniel

was able to hear and obey the voice of God that gave him direction. Obedience comes from our ability to listen. We can also learn how God speaks to us through fellowship with each other. Each generation has its own wisdom to share regarding what God's voice sounds like, metaphorically speaking. We can mutually teach each other what His Word means to us and how we are obedient to Him.

Part of obedience is knowing when and how to listen and knowing when and how to act. In a world filled with noise and distractions, can we truly focus on the only thing that matters? Can we act in community to show our obedience?

After knowing the context and personal faith differences of the person you are having intergenerational communication with, it is very important to join in community with action. We have discussed that obedience is seen through action, so obey together. Remain set apart from the world. Do things together—church, celebrations, prayer, Bible study. Be active in reading, discussing, understanding, and practicing the principles in God's Word together. Take action.

Action could be as simple as praying together or reading a section of Scripture. But it can also be as complex as outreach to the community, state, nation, and world. In the book of Matthew, Yeshua calls us to go out. He is calling us to take action by teaching others about obedience and all that He spoke about (Matthew 28:19–20). It is important to participate in community together, as an intergenerational pair, because in this way, we have the capacity to reach a wider array of people than if we are acting alone.

FIVE
DANIEL HAD DEVOTION

STICKING TO THE SET-APART LIFE

Linda

Read Daniel 1:3–7:

> Then the king told Ashpenaz, the chief of
> his officials, to bring in some of the sons of
> Israel, including some of the royal family and
> of the nobles, youths in whom there was no
> impairment, who were good-looking, suitable for
> instruction in every kind of expertise, endowed
> with understanding and discerning knowledge,
> and who had ability to serve in the king's court;
> and he ordered Ashpenaz to teach them the
> literature and language of the Chaldeans. The
> king also allotted for them a daily ration from
> the king's choice food and from the wine which
> he drank, and ordered that they be educated

for three years, at the end of which they were to
enter the king's personal service. Now among
them from the sons of Judah were Daniel,
Hananiah, Mishael and Azariah. Then the
commander of the officials assigned new names
to them; and to Daniel he assigned the name
Belteshazzar, to Hananiah Shadrach, to Mishael
Meshach and to Azariah Abed-nego.

As we have already seen, Daniel and his three friends were
ripped from their homes when they were teenagers. At the time
of this writing I have two grandsons and two granddaughters who
are fifteen years old. I cannot imagine them being in that kind of
traumatic situation. Daniel and his three friends would have lost
everything: friends, family, home, wealth, prestige, social status,
schooling, security, health, food, and future. Normal life was taken
away.

I am sure Daniel wondered, *Where is Elohim? Where is the Lord?*
He might have been asking, *Are we truly the chosen people? Where
is His guidance and direction? Are we just supposed to assimilate into
this godforsaken culture?* I am sure he was questioning whether the
teaching he received throughout the fifteen or sixteen years of his
life was going to sustain him, whether his devotion would remain
strong.

Because he was a part of the nobility, he and his friends would
have been very well educated and taken care of. They most likely
had many Bible verses committed to memory. But on their way
to Babylon, that status would have been stripped from them,

making them nothing more than slaves. The family treasures they were carrying would be taken from them as soon as they reached Babylon.

They traveled a thousand miles on foot to the pagan city. Babylon was a city of idolatry, murder, and hate. It was filled with evil people. Daniel would have been hungry (perhaps for the first time in his life), uncomfortable, tired, thirsty, alone, and abandoned. The beauty and serenity of the temple, gone. Feasts and celebrations, gone. Security, gone. The happy times, gone. Normal was gone, but he remained devoted.

When the children of Jerusalem arrived in Babylon, the culture of Babylon was thrust on them. Even their names were changed (Daniel 1:6–7). Daniel (which means "God is my judge") became Belteshazzar, which means "Baal, protect him." Hananiah (which means "Jehovah has been gracious") became Shadrach, which means "the command of Aku." Mishael (which means "who is what God is?") became Meshach, which means "who is what Aku is?" Azariah (which means "Jehovah has helped") became Abed-nego, which means "servant of Nabo."[1]

Here is a thought-provoking question. Did you know the Jewish names of all four of these children? Did you know their Babylonian names? While many people know Daniel's name, I found myself having to look up the Hebrew names of the other three. Why is it that we all know the Babylonian names better? The Babylonian names are not their God-given names.

Read Daniel 1:8–16:

> But Daniel made up his mind that he would
> not defile himself with the king's choice food
> or with the wine which he drank; so he sought
> permission from the commander of the officials
> that he might not defile himself. Now God
> granted Daniel favor and compassion in the
> sight of the commander of the officials. The
> commander of the officials said to Daniel, "I am
> afraid of my lord the king, who has allotted your
> food and your drink; for why should he see your
> faces looking gaunt in comparison to the youths
> who are your own age? Then you would make
> me forfeit my head to the king." But Daniel said
> to the overseer whom the commander of the
> officials had appointed over Daniel, Hananiah,
> Mishael, and Azariah, "Please put your servants
> to the test for ten days, and let us be given some
> vegetables to eat and water to drink. Then let our
> appearance be examined in your presence and
> the appearance of the youths who are eating the
> king's choice food; and deal with your servants
> according to what you see."
>
> So he listened to them in this matter, and put
> them to the test them for ten days. At the end
> of ten days their appearance seemed better,
> and they were fatter than all the youths who
> had been eating the king's choice food. So the
> overseer continued to withhold their choice food

and the wine they were to drink, and kept giving
them vegetables.

There is a misconception that the young men are advocating
for a plant-based diet when they did not want to eat the meat and
wine the king provided. But why did they refuse it? In verse 8, the
terminology used to explain why Daniel refused the king's food is
"that he might not defile himself." This same kind of language is
used in Leviticus 11:43–44: "Do not make yourselves detestable
through any of the swarming things that swarm; and you shall
not make yourselves unclean with them so that you become
unclean. For I am the LORD your God. Consecrate yourselves
therefore, and be holy, because I am holy. And you shall not make
yourselves unclean with any of the swarming things that swarm
on the earth."

The entirety of Leviticus 11 is the instructions Yahweh gave to
His people regarding what was clean and unclean to eat, as well as
what made someone clean and unclean regarding handling flesh.
Read all of Leviticus 11 to get a full understanding of the kinds of
things Yahweh asked His people to do.

Each of these commands was given with the intention of
teaching His people how to live a healthy life, avoiding disease and
illness, and to be set apart. There is even a section regarding storing
flesh in earthenware vessels. God's people were commanded to
break that earthenware vessel after it came in contact with unclean
flesh. Modern science has proven that the bacteria, or things that
make you sick, cannot be washed out of pots like that, something
they would not have been able to prove at the time the Torah (the

Law) was given. This is another way Yahweh's instructions protected His people.

At the end of Leviticus 11, Elohim commands His people not to defile themselves and be set apart. When Daniel and his three friends chose not to eat and drink what the king gave them, they were showing their devotion by following Yahweh's commands given in Leviticus 11. They were being set apart from the nations who freely ate and changed the definition of "food" to include what Elohim defined as *not* food.

The clean food and drink spoken of in Leviticus 11 are also known as "kosher" to Yahweh's people. Daniel challenged the Babylonians about this kosher diet in a way that was also peace seeking. He was very wise to find the middle ground. He essentially said, "Don't make us eat this meat, and we will look healthier, which will look good for you as well as us." He was able to honor the culture that was important to him, which God had called them to do, and still be peace seekers among his captors. He did it in a humble, not dramatic, way. This is also an admirable quality.

Ultimately, the young adults refused the non-kosher meat and the wine of the king. Granted, it would have been very unusual for them to refuse the wine in particular. They had been drinking wine since they were thirteen years old or younger. Most of the biblical feasts have an abundance of wine, so we know that these young men were not teetotalers. Why refuse the wine of Babylon?

My husband and I once went to six intensive classes on wine and how to grow the vine. They were the best Bible study classes I have ever attended. The Scriptures are filled with references to the fruit of the vine; John 15 is one example. The wine of Babylon was probably clarified or filtered through the gelatin of pork products. A lot of the wine that is sold in the US is clarified this way. Their wine might have been stored in pig stomachs because they did not have glass bottles at the time. So, if you are allergic to pork, which a lot of my family is, then a glass of the wrong kind of wine can make you really sick.

Daniel and his friends remained devoted and true to their beliefs despite the pressure from their new home and new "masters." This is another key element of their strength. They did not allow themselves to be indoctrinated into the cultural elements they were brought into; they remained set apart. In this way they displayed devotion to the life God called them to live.

THE FIERY FURNACE

Linda

❧

Read the story of the fiery furnace in Daniel 3:9–30. Daniel's three friends were challenged again. Nebuchadnezzar was so impressed by Daniel's interpretation of a dream he had that he made a gold statue to represent himself as the head of all the idols. This statue was huge, ninety feet tall by nine feet wide (Daniel 3:1). Nebuchadnezzar commanded the people to worship this statue. Everyone was to fall down and worship or else be thrown into the fiery furnace. Everyone did fall down, except the three friends. It is worth noting that Daniel was not in the area at this time, or else there would have been four, not three, refusing to fall.

The young men again showed their unwavering devotion to God. They had been taught Exodus 20:3–6 from childhood: "You shall have no other gods before Me. You shall not make for yourself an idol, or any likeness of what is in heaven above or on the earth beneath, or in the water under the earth. You shall not worship them nor serve them; for I, the LORD your God, am a jealous God, inflicting the punishment of the fathers on the children, on the third and the fourth generations of those who hate Me, but showing favor to thousands, to those who love Me and keep My commandments." They were not to worship or fall down to an idol. They stated that God was more than able to save them, but even if He chose not to save them, they would not serve or worship an image.

This same phrase, "but if not," was used in WWII by those fighting against Germany's invasion of England. A British naval officer used it in a distress call back to England.[2] The message said they would fight and, with God's help, win. But if not, they would still refuse to bow down to the utter tyranny of Germany's power.

It is amazing that the officer said, "But if not." Many who heard his words at that time understood what he was subtly saying.

Danigirlsart

As was generally true in biblical times, people knew the Word and would have known the story of the fiery furnace. God would have had to intervene on behalf of the English people and save them. These soldiers were looking at death and not blinking.

We know how the story in Daniel ends. There were four in the fire: three young men and a preincarnation appearance of Yeshua. The young men came out unscathed; the only thing that burned were the ropes binding them.

We also know how the other story ends. England and the allies defeated Germany. In both cases God provided a way out. "But if not" became "God fought and won."

As believers we bow to *no* man or organization. We only bow our knee to the Lord. Make up your mind now to follow this rule. People in power will pressure you to bow down to their evil gods and ideology, and they won't be as obvious as giant gold statues. We must be diligent in examining whether ideas, movements, and beliefs line up with the Word of God. You belong to the King of the universe; you are His child. Stand up, stand up. Stand up and praise your Lord.

CONNECTING THROUGH REFLECTIONS ON DEVOTION

Linda

◦

When it comes to devotion in intergenerational communication, there are two aspects to consider: (1) We should show devotion to each other by mirroring the love our Father shows us, and (2) our devotion to our Father should be evident to each other. Mirroring the love our Father shows us to others is an important goal when connecting through intergenerational communication. But what does that look like?

Have you ever seen a beautiful sunrise or sunset or looked at a starry night or a field of wildflowers and just thought, *Wow!* Has the Lord caused you to be so filled with joy that tears came to your eyes? What about the first time you saw your newborn child or a new grandchild? The Lord looks at us like that, His face shining with love and care. He sees us through the eyes of His Son, not the eyes of the world.

You are loved. John 3:16 will probably be very familiar to you, but if not, please take a look and finish this verse: "For God so loved the world that_____."

With a foundation of love in an intergenerational connection, it is easier to share experiences and more rewarding to feel the love and acceptance of the other. "We love, because He first loved us" (1 John 4:19).

When it comes to how we show devotion to each other, we can look to the Bible to see examples of how to love Yahweh. A great story of love and devotion in the Bible is the Son's love for His heavenly Father. Messiah said in the garden of Gethsemane, "Not my will, but thine, be done" (Luke 22:42 KJV). This is an example of absolute willingness to follow, no matter what will happen.

To love the heavenly Father and His Son is to follow Him when you are on the mountaintop surrounded by joy and peace, but also when you are in the valley of the shadow of death (Psalm 23).

We see evidence of Daniel's devotion to God by analyzing the actions that he took. What actions do you take that would be evidence of your devotion to God? How can an intergenerational communication relationship foster devotion? It may start more personally but can be encouraged by connecting with one another. One thought to consider when analyzing whether your devotion is able to be seen by others is whether God truly holds supremacy in your life.

Each generation must ask the question, who is God? Is He the supreme ruler of the universe? Or is He like Santa Claus? It is easy to fall into the trap of "I want, I want" when it comes to Yahweh. But God's intended relationship with us is much deeper than that. Rather, we must allow God to hold supremacy over our lives because He loves us.

We have all experienced times in our lives when our wants invade our perception of God. Consequently, we allow the world to hold supremacy over us. Instead of surrendering ourselves wholly to God, we tighten our grip on our fleeting hope of control. We cannot be devoted to the world; we must be devoted to God.

Daniel did not allow a king or political job to have control over his life. Rather, he surrendered his will to God's and recognized God's supremacy over himself. He recognized the love that God had for him, the same love God has for us.

Reflect on your own devotion in your life. In what ways have you devoted your life to God? What holds supremacy over you? Would the person you are holding an intergenerational conversation with see your devotion to God and have it be an encouragement to them? These are important things to consider.

SIX
DANIEL HAD KNOWLEDGE

THE IMPORTANCE OF KNOWLEDGE

Linda

One characteristic of Daniel that is even less tangible than some of his others is knowledge. By this word, I mean that Daniel had a strong biblical background. We have already mentioned that Daniel grew up in nobility and had access to the Torah. He likely made use of that access and committed large parts of it to memory. Even though he was young, I believe that if he would have been questioned regarding the background of his faith, he would have had no problem answering those questions.

That being said, we *know* that his faith was questioned. He was carted off to a brand-new culture where no teacher was around to hold his hand or tell him right from wrong. He already knew right from wrong and the foundational elements of his relationship with God because of his background. How strong is your biblical knowledge? Could you survive the trip to Babylon and subsequent life in a foreign culture based on what you know of the Bible right now? This is a hard question to consider.

Years ago, when my twin grandsons were four, one twin, Ethan, found a small plastic bead on the ground at his daycare center. This bead, according to Ethan, looked exactly like the small fish egg that produced the loving character Nemo in the cartoon movie *Finding Nemo*.

Ethan was convinced that this was a fish egg, so he put it in his pocket and carried it home and put it in a clear plastic glass filled with water.

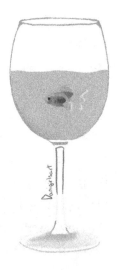

His twin brother, Austin, and older sister, Kaitlyn (age seven at the time), tried to convince him that this was not a fish egg. This ridicule continued for some time, but Ethan would not be moved.

He was sure that all it took was time and patience and a fish would appear.

It was around this time that the kids watched God's magnificent creation of a butterfly. They all saw the green caterpillar become the cocoon and a majestic monarch appear. What a wonderful experience, and an even better transformation for the kids to witness.

So, Ethan waited—one week, two weeks. In the meantime, his aunt came for a visit. Ethan's mom and aunt decided that they might just "help nature along." They went to Walmart and bought the smallest red fish I had ever seen and replaced the red bead with the new fish. Ethan's mom then told him to get something off his dresser where the fish was.

In a short time, they heard screaming coming from the room. Ethan had found the fish. Hearing the screaming coming from the room, the other kids and adults, with camera in hand, ran to the room. Kaitlyn, our problem solver, was instantly worried about how they would feed it and where it would live because it couldn't live in a plastic glass forever. Her aunt assured her that she had bought everything this fish could possibly need.

The comment from Austin was priceless. He said, "Well, dude, I was wrong. I really thought that it was a plastic bead, but I guess I was wrong." Kaitlyn was not convinced; it was a plastic bead found on the ground—it was not a fish egg. She did not know how this fish got there, but she was not going to be fooled.

Ethan was beside himself with joy. It was his fish, and he named it Ethan Bobbie. He called me so excited and told me what happened. I said, "Ethan, what are you going to do with the fish?" I really wanted him to tell me about the new aquarium that his aunt had bought, but he said, "I will keep it until it dies."

I could talk about childlike faith and how precious it is, but I want to zero in on the reaction of Austin and Kaitlyn. In Mark 13:20–23 God, through the Holy Spirit, tells us that in the end of time, during the tribulation, the Antichrist is going to produce miracles through the forces of evil. These miracles are going to be so outstanding that they will possibly fool even the elect.

Are we going to be like Ethan and Austin and be tricked with our eyes—as seen in Colossians 2:8, which cautions us, "See to it that there is no one who takes you captive through philosophy and empty deception in accordance with human tradition, in accordance with the elementary principles of the world, rather than in accordance with Christ"—or are we going to be like Kaitlyn and say, "I know what I know, and it's a plastic bead"?

Do you know what you know? Are you 100 percent assured of the truth of the Word of God? Do you know John 14:6, which reminds us Jesus is the way, the only way? Kaitlyn called me and said, "Grandma, it was just a bead." She was trying to convince me. We as Christians need to convince others.

We must stand on biblical truth, no matter what the world throws at us. My grandson Austin relied only on sight. He saw a fish, so in his eyes the bead must have been a fish egg. Kaitlyn relied on past knowledge to understand that the bead could not turn into a fish, even though her eyes were seeing it. Build your foundation on biblical truth.

Then Ethan came home with a yellow bead . . .

DANIEL, HANANIAH, MISHAEL, AND AZARIAH'S FOUNDATION IN THE WORD OF GOD

Linda

❧

What Scripture did these four young men have? They did not have the New Testament, which is often the starting place for new believers today, so what did they look to for written truth? What did they memorize, meditate on, and read three times a day (Daniel 6:10)?

How did they know about God, His love for them, and their people's history? Daniel and the other captive Israelites would have carried many ancient scrolls into Babylon. They would have had access to the Torah, Genesis through Deuteronomy, all the Psalms and Proverbs, and many of the major and minor prophets. For proof of this, remember that Daniel was reading Jeremiah 25:11–12 in Daniel 9:2.

What Old Testament books and verses would have greatly encouraged Daniel? The psalms of David would have comforted him as he traveled to and lived in Babylon. Maybe Psalm 23, which begins with "The LORD is my shepherd," was one of his favorites.

Maybe Job 19:25–27 gave him great comfort: "Yet as for me, I know that my Redeemer lives, and at the last, He will take His stand on the earth. Even after my skin is destroyed, yet from my flesh I will see God, whom I, on my part, shall behold for myself, and whom my eyes will see, and not another. My heart faints within me!"

Daniel and his friends would have certainly been aware of all the verses and may have even put the whole Torah to memory. The Old Testament probably comforted and sustained the captive Israelites during their seventy years of exile.

We will probably not be kidnapped and taken to Babylon, but what verses do you know that will help in times of stress and persecution?

Kaitlyn and I have selected a few verses below that display foundational concepts we feel are important to know, meditate on, and memorize. The concepts include the following:

- **The Son.** Yeshua is the Son of our heavenly Father sent to save the world. He lived a perfect life but died for our sins, was buried, and rose again on the third day. In Hebrew, Yeshua means "salvation." Eternal life is through belief in the name of the only Son of God—He is salvation.
- **The Word.** It is important to believe the Bible is the Word of God. The Bible is Basic Instructions Before Leaving Earth. Yeshua is called the Word in John 1:1.
- **The Holy Spirit.** The Holy Spirit is the messenger of God. The Spirit comforts, teaches, and reminds us of the power, strength, and creativity of the Father and His Son. We are sealed (protected) by the Spirit.

- **Loving.** We are to turn fully to the Lord to love Him with all our heart, soul, mind, and strength because He is a worthy God.
- **Believing.** Belief is the cornerstone of one who follows the Lord. By faith we are able to come to the Father through Yeshua. We must believe that He is the sovereign Creator of the universe and that we can rest fully in knowing that everything, the good things in life as well as the bad, will be held in His hands.
- **Confessing.** Confession means to turn away from the sin that is preventing us from having fellowship with the Lord. By taking this first step, we open the door for our merciful God to show His forgiveness and repair the mistakes we have made.
- **Following.** The Holy Spirit's direction through the Bible can help us identify how we're called to follow the Lord. When we follow God, we can also proclaim our faith to others.

The following verses, of course, are not all-inclusive, and you may have many other verses that you love. But we feel that these verses embody some of the basic building blocks of faith in Yahweh. Please use the space given to write your thoughts on each verse as you read through. Take the time to meditate on each one.

The Son

"For God so loved the world, that He gave His only Son, so that everyone who believes in Him will not perish, but have eternal life. For God did not send the Son into the world to judge the world, but so that the world might be saved through Him. The one who believes in Him is not judged; the one who does not believe has been judged already, because he has not believed in the name of the only Son of God" (John 3:16–18).

"For I handed down to you as of first importance what I also received, that Christ died for our sins according to the Scriptures, and that He was buried, and that He was raised on the third day according to the Scriptures" (1 Corinthians 15:3–4).

"And there is salvation in no one else; for there is no other name under heaven that has been given among mankind by which we must be saved" (Acts 4:12).

"For the wages of sin is death; but the gift of God is eternal life through Christ Jesus our Lord" (Romans 6:23 KJV).

"For there is one God, and one mediator also between God and mankind, the man Christ Jesus, who gave Himself as a ransom for all, the testimony given at the proper time" (1 Timothy 2:5–6).

The Word

"All Scripture is inspired by God and beneficial for teaching, for rebuke, for correction, for training in righteousness; so that the man or woman of God may be fully capable, equipped for every good work." (2 Timothy 3:16–17)

"In the beginning was the Word, and the Word was with God, and the Word was God" (John 1:1).

The Holy Spirit

"But the Helper, the Holy Spirit whom the Father will send in My name, He will teach you all things, and remind you of all that I said to you" (John 14:26).

"In Him, you also, after listening to the message of truth, the gospel of your salvation—having also believed, you were sealed in Him with the Holy Spirit of the promise, who is a first installment of our inheritance, in regard to the redemption of God's own possession, to the praise of His glory" (Ephesians 1:13–14).

Loving

"Worthy are You, our Lord and our God, to receive glory and honor and power; for You created all things, and because of Your will they existed, and were created" (Revelation 4:11).

"Jesus answered, 'The foremost is, "HEAR, ISRAEL! THE LORD YOUR GOD IS ONE; AND YOU SHALL LOVE THE LORD WITH ALL YOUR HEART, AND WITH ALL YOUR SOUL, AND WITH ALL YOUR MIND, AND WITH ALL YOUR STRENGTH." The second is this: "YOU SHALL LOVE YOUR NEIGHBOR AS YOURSELF." There is no other commandment greater than these'" (Mark 12:29–31).

"Hear, Israel! The LORD is our God, the LORD is one! And you shall love the LORD your God with all your heart and with all your soul and with all your strength. These words, which I am commanding you today, shall be on your heart" (Deuteronomy 6:4–6).

"And we know that God causes all things to work together for good to those who love God, to those who are called according to His purpose" (Romans 8:28).

Believing

"Now faith is the certainty of things hoped for, a proof of things not seen" (Hebrews 11:1).

"Jesus said to him, 'I am the way, and the truth, and the life; no one comes to the Father except through Me"(John 14:6).

"So faith comes from hearing, and hearing by the word of Christ" (Romans 10:17).

"For I am not ashamed of the gospel, for it is the power of God for salvation to everyone who believes, to the Jew first and also to the Greek. For in it the righteousness of God is revealed from faith to faith; as it is written: 'BUT THE RIGHTEOUS ONE WILL LIVE BY FAITH'" (Romans 1:16–17).

Confessing

"But what does it say? 'THE WORD IS NEAR YOUR, IN YOUR MOUTH AND IN YOUR HEART'—that is, the word of faith which we are preaching, that if you confess with your mouth Jesus as Lord, and believe in your heart that God raised Him from the dead, you will be saved; for with the heart a person believes, resulting in righteousness, and with the mouth he confesses, resulting in salvation" (Romans 10:8–10).

"If we say that we have no sin, we are deceiving ourselves and the truth is not in us. If we confess our sins, He is faithful and righteous, so that He will forgive us our sins and cleanse us from all unrighteousness" (1 John 1:8–9).

Following

"And He said to them, 'Follow Me, and I will make you fishers of people'" (Matthew 4:19).

"And without faith it is impossible to please Him, for the one who comes to God must believe that He exists, and that He proves to be One who rewards those who seek Him" (Hebrews 11:6).

CONNECTING THROUGH REFLECTIONS ON KNOWLEDGE

Linda

❧

My oldest daughter went on a South African safari photoshoot. I enjoyed the magnificent pictures of lions, cheetahs, leopards, elephants, and zebras that she took. I especially loved the stories of the people who live there.

One story was about how they protected their children from wild animals while they played outside. The parents put a ring of fire made of lanterns around their children. The children then played only inside the ring of lanterns. The children were reminded over and over again to play only in this area. A child leaving the protection of the fire would be easy prey for the wild animals of the area. One day a six-year-old boy left the security and safety of the ring. Within minutes a leopard descended on him and proceeded to drag him away by his head, neck, and back. His parents heard the screaming and were able to save their son by snatching him out of the mouth of this huge cat.

So why did he leave the safety of the ring? Didn't he think that his parents were telling the truth when they warned him? Was he determined to do what he wanted, or was he just too young to grasp the danger? We will never know the answer.

What we do know is he strayed from the safety of the ring of fire. Do we have a ring of fire around us? Do we have places we should not go, things we should not do, lines we should not cross? As a Christian I believe the answer is yes. The Bible is filled with warnings; the Lord does not want us to be destroyed or killed by the lion (i.e., Satan) who prowls around seeking to destroy our lives. "Be of sober spirit, be on the alert. Your adversary, the devil, prowls around like a roaring lion, seeking someone to devour" (1 Peter 5:8).

Don't venture outside the ring of fire, the ring of safety, that the Bible describes for us. Don't be lax in knowing the truth within God's Word. In an intergenerational conversation we should encourage each other to know what is right and what is wrong. Remain set apart; remain in His Word. While this will be a mutual encouragement, it falls to the older to teach and the younger to be willing to learn.

Think of Eli and Samuel (1 Samuel 3). The high priest at Shiloh, Eli, cared for and raised the very small child, Samuel. Samuel had been left at the temple at probably the age of five years old by his mother, Hannah, and father. This was the result of a vow Hannah had made to the Lord. The boy was to grow up in the temple and serve the Lord and high priest all of his days.

We see a very old man and highly respected priest of God mentoring and teaching this small child. He was like a grandfather to this young child, raising him in the Lord.

Consider also Paul and Timothy (1 Timothy 1:1-2). The apostle Paul, a very knowledgeable Hebrew rabbi, instructed a young man,

Timothy, and taught him sound doctrines of the Word of God. Where did Timothy first learn about the Scriptures and the Lord? It was from his grandmother, Lois, and his mother, Eunice. This is family passing down the knowledge of the Lord.

There are Naomi and Ruth (see the book of Ruth). We see the older woman, Naomi, teaching God's Word to her younger daughter-in-law, Ruth. It is evident they loved each other and cared for each other. God's love and protection are woven into this beautiful story.

The New Testament calls older women to be sanctifed (set apart) in holy behavior, not addicted to wine, and to be teachers of the Word. They are to train the younger women to love their husbands and families and care for them (Titus 2:3–5).

That said, in each of these stories the older, more knowledgeable person mentored, discipled, and taught the younger. And in each of these relationships the younger was willing to learn from the older mentor.

This concept can also apply in reverse. The younger may have a greater knowledge of worldly trends that brings perspective and balance to the wisdom of the older. The younger generation tends to be more in tune with social surroundings as evidenced by social media. These unique perspectives can be utilized in an intergenerational conversation to provide the older generation with a viewpoint on present culture. This is especially relevant when attempting to reach a broader, more diverse population.

Ultimately, God's Spirit protects us and leads us in the right direction if we choose to listen. Effective communication across generations allows us to share our knowledge. We must strive to become purposeful, spiritually oriented, and humble each in our own way. We do not always know everything, but that is okay. We must challenge one another to better understand God's will for us.

Discussing true biblical knowledge and engaging in conversations about broader culture will take some effort, but the reward of outreach and growth in knowledge is eternal.

SEVEN

DANIEL HAD PRAYER

THE LIONS' DEN
AND THE ACTS OF PRAYER

Kaitlyn

W hen most people hear the name Daniel in reference to the Bible, they think of the story of Daniel in the lions' den. We have already talked about Daniel's faith in that story, but there is another aspect of his character that is illuminated by Daniel's brush with death in the lions' den. That character trait is prayerfulness. Read Daniel 6:1–28.

The first thing to recognize in this chapter is that Daniel had a position of authority above all others (besides the king) because God allowed him to succeed and earn the attention and trust of the king (v. 3). As we have seen through Daniel's upbringing and young life in Babylon, he was not one to stray away from God, even when pressured to do so by others. Throughout the Bible we see examples of God rewarding or recognizing this type of devotion. God rewarded Daniel's strong faith and obedience with success among the nations. Elohim was faithful in protecting Daniel when his whole world was being torn apart—literally—and Daniel hunkered down in his faith and prayed and obeyed the whole time.

In verses 4–9, the corrupt and jealous men of the king's court realized that the only way to get rid of Daniel was to attack his faith. They manipulated the king into signing a decree making it illegal to live the life of prayer Daniel was used to living. Afterward, when Daniel's first response was to continue praying, obeying, and living the life he was called to live in Babylon, God was steadfast in rewarding Daniel by keeping him safe through the punishment and placing him in a position of power.

Daniel was saved from the lions, but what happened to the men who tricked King Darius into throwing Daniel into the den? "The king then gave orders, and they brought those men who had maliciously accused Daniel, and they threw them, their children, and their wives into the lions' den; and they had not reached the bottom of the den before the lions overpowered them and crushed all their bones" (Daniel 6:24).

These men and their families were viciously punished for their wrongdoing against Daniel.

King Darius knew that the God of Daniel was powerful and merciful. He probably had heard about the fiery furnace as well as King Nebuchadnezzar's episode in the field with the cattle (more will be said of this incident in chapter 8). He might have even seen the writing on the wall (see chapter 8) as he came into the king's palace to take over.

After seeing Elohim's compassion on Daniel, knowing this mighty God had mercy, what did Darius do? He killed the innocent infants and children. I fault him for that; leave the kids out of this mess! Darius was a prideful man, then a humbled angry man, then a man full of vengeance, destruction, and murder.

King Darius may have been an indecisive type of king before the lion incident, but afterward I see him as a strong and violent leader who would never be fooled again. His subjects, and the leaders in his government gained new fear of him. His word was absolute law.

There is also something to be said of God's willingness to give Daniel this position of authority to benefit the whole land as well. God allowed Daniel to rise to the top and be loved by the king, which put the king in the position to recognize God's power through Daniel's rescue in the lions' den and proclaim God as the only god to worship. If we could ask Daniel what he thought would have been the outcome before any of that happened, he probably couldn't have guessed the result.

Is your world being torn apart? It often feels this way, even if we don't have people invading our homes or we aren't physically defenseless, staring down a bunch of hungry lions. How did Daniel respond to the trials he was given? He prayed. He had a strong relationship and trust in God, so he prayed. Prayer is the backbone to faith, as we have seen throughout Daniel. Daniel also gives us the perfect lesson in how to pray.

Read Daniel 9:3–19 below. This is Daniel's prayer after he discovers in the writings of Jeremiah that Israel's captivity in Babylon was drawing to an end. Analyzing this prayer, it is clear

he uses the format called ACTS. Underline and label each of these
sections according to ACTS:

>A – Adoration (vv. 3–4)
>C – Confession (vv. 5–13)
>T – Thanksgiving (vv. 14–15)
>S – Supplication (vv. 16–19)

So I gave my attention to the Lord God, to
seek Him by prayer and pleading, with fasting,
sackcloth, and ashes. I prayed to the LORD
my God and confessed, and said, "Oh, Lord,
the great and awesome God, who keeps His
covenant and faithfulness for those who love
Him and keep His commandments, we have
sinned, we have done wrong, and acted wickedly
and rebelled, even turning aside from Your
commandments and ordinances. Moreover, we
have not listened to Your servants the prophets,
who spoke in Your name to our kings, our
leaders, our fathers, and all the people of the
land.

"Righteousness belongs to You, Lord, but to us
open shame, as it is this day—
to the men of Judah, the inhabitants of
Jerusalem, and all Israel, those who are nearby
and those who are far away in all the countries
to which You have driven them, because of their
unfaithful deeds which they have committed
against You. Open shame belongs to us, LORD,
to our kings, our leaders, and our fathers,

because we have sinned against You. To the Lord
our God belong compassion and forgiveness,
because we have rebelled against Him; and we
have not obeyed the voice of the LORD our God,
to walk in His teachings which He set before
us through His servants the prophets. Indeed,
all Israel has violated Your Law and turned
aside, not obeying Your voice; so the curse has
gushed forth on us, along with the oath which is
written in the Law of Moses the servant of God,
because we have sinned against Him. So He
has confirmed His words which He had spoken
against us and against our rulers who ruled us,
to bring on us great disaster; for under the entire
heaven there has not been done anything like
what was done in Jerusalem. Just as it is written
in the Law of Moses, all this disaster has come
on us; yet we have not sought the favor of the
LORD our God by turning from our wrongdoing
and giving attention to Your truth. So the LORD
has kept the disaster in store and brought it
on us; for the LORD our God is righteous with
respect to all His deeds which He has done, but
we have not obeyed His voice.

"And now, Lord, our God, You who brought
Your people out of the land of
Egypt with a mighty hand and made a name
for Yourself, as it is this day—we have sinned,
we have been wicked. Lord, in accordance with
all Your righteous acts, let now Your anger and

Your wrath turn away from Your city Jerusalem,
Your holy mountain; for because of our sins and
the wrongdoings of our fathers, Jerusalem and
Your people have become an object of taunting
to all those around us. So now, our God, listen to
the prayer of Your servant and to his pleas, and
for Your sake, Lord, let Your face shine on Your
desolate sanctuary. My God, incline Your ear and
hear! Open Your eyes and see our desolations
and the city which is called by Your name; for we
are not presenting our pleas before You based on
any merits of our own, but based on Your great
compassion. Lord, hear! Lord, forgive! Lord, listen
and take action! For Your own sake, my God, do
not delay, because Your city and Your people are
called by Your name." (Daniel 9:3–19)

Where else in the Bible are we taught how to pray? Yeshua gives
us what is formally known as the Lord's Prayer. This prayer, while
shorter, contains similar elements to Daniel's prayer in Daniel 9 and
follows ACTS, albeit in a different order. Read Matthew 6:9–13.

Adoration
"Pray, then, in this way:
'Our Father who is in heaven,
Hallowed be Your name.
Your kingdom come.
Your will be done,
On earth as it is in heaven.'"
(Matthew 6:9–10)

Supplication

"Give us this day our daily bread."
(Matthew 6:11)

Confession

"And forgive us our debts,
as we also have forgiven our debtors."
(Matthew 6:12)

Supplication

"And do not lead us into temptation,
but deliver us from evil."
(Matthew 6:13)

Thanksgiving

"For Yours is the kingdom and the power
and the glory forever. Amen."
(Matthew 6:13 NKJV)

We can use this ACTS model to shape our own prayers as well. It is also important to note that Daniel specifically prayed for his nation. Are you praying for your nation? Even though the United States seems to be very divided and people do not agree on our leaders, it is still our job to pray for them and to ask that God keeps His hands on the nation as a whole.

There is certainly no right way to pray. This is a prompt that I use to guide my prayers, and I would encourage you, dear reader, to use this prompt as well.

A – Adoration - "Father God, you are amazing . . ."

C – Confession - "I have sinned . . ."

T – Thanksgiving - "Thank you for blessing me in
this way . . ."

S – Supplication - "I would like to pray for . . ."

1. Global concerns/leaders
2. National concerns/leaders
3. Local community
4. Friends
5. Family
6. Yourself

POSITIONS OF PRAYER

Linda

~

Read John 8:1–11. Pay attention to the language used to describe the physical posture of each person. Put yourself in the crowd.

You are *sitting* in a crowd, and Yeshua comes and sits down with you to teach you (v. 2).

The scribes and Pharisees bring a woman caught in adultery and *set* her *down* with the crowd and Yeshua (v. 3).

After the scribes and Pharisees condemn her with adultery, they challenge Yeshua with a question (vv. 4–5).

Yeshua, from a *sitting* position, *bends down* and writes on the ground (v. 6).

Then he *stands* (with authority) and says, "He who is without sin among you, let him be the first to throw a stone at her" (v. 7).

Yeshua again *stoops* down and writes on the ground (v. 8).

The accusers leaves; Yeshua is *sitting,* and the woman is now *standing* in the midst of the crowd (v. 9).

"And straightening up, Jesus said to her, 'Woman, where are they? Did no one condemn you?' She said, 'No one, Lord.' And

Jesus said, 'I do not condemn you, either. Go. From now on do not sin any longer'" (vv. 10–11).

I encourage you to take note of the posture of people in the Bible. Are they sitting, standing, kneeling, or have they fallen on their faces? Like many principles of culture, each of these positions indicates more than just their comfort level.

In the Bible, standing means authority, sitting means one's work is done, fellowship, or comfort; kneeling means worship; and falling on one's face means worship with fear.

Here are some additional examples of kneeling in the Bible:

- Yeshua knelt while praying at the Mount of Olives before His crucifixion (Luke 22:39–41).
- Demon-possessed man knelt before Yeshua (Matthew 17:14).
- The rich young ruler knelt before Yeshua (Mark 10:17).
- In the future every knee shall bow and every tongue will confess that Yeshua is Lord (Romans 14:11; Philippians 2:10–11; Isaiah 45:23).

Here are some examples of sitting:

- Yeshua sits on the right hand of power (Matthew 26:64).
- Many times in the book of Revelation the words sitting, sit, or sat, are used, denoting completion or rest. I challenge you to read Revelation and underline those words.

Several examples of standing in the Bible include Yeshua standing in Revelation 3:20, 20:12, 7:9, and 4:1.

An example of falling down in worship was when John fell as a dead man when he saw Yeshua as King in power (Revelation 1:17).

In Nehemiah, the wall of the city (Jerusalem) was completed in just fifty-two days. Nehemiah 8:5 gives us a very interesting story. When the Torah (law) was opened to be read to the people, they *stood* up, *lifting* their hands, *bowing* their faces to the ground. This was a display of absolute reverence and worship of the Lord of the universe.

In what position did Daniel most often pray? Daniel's beloved Jerusalem, where the temple of Elohim was, where his home and family were, where his friends and schools of learning resided, was five hundred miles (as the crow flies) straight west from Babylon. As we've said before, the actual trip to Babylon was a thousand miles taking roads that went straight north, then east.

Daniel 6:10 states that Daniel lived in a house with an upper room that had east-facing windows toward Jerusalem. Three times a day you could find Daniel *kneeling* down and giving thanks to his God. Morning, noon, and night, day after day, year after year, decade after decade, for seventy years of captivity. Morning, noon, and night were also the times of animal sacrifice at the Temple Mount in Jerusalem. These sacrifices obviously only occurred when the temple was still standing, before the destruction and fire.

When Daniel looked out these windows that faced east, he would have been turning his back on many satanic temples in Babylon. We have discussed gods and goddesses on several pages in this book, but I want to emphasize one god in particular; that is the god Molech. Molech was a Babylonian god who required millions of infant and child sacrifices. The idea of any human sacrifice is loathsome to the heavenly Father of the universe. As Leviticus 18:21 states, "You shall not give any of your children to offer them to Molech, nor shall you profane the name of your God; I am the Lord."

Molech's temple was embedded on top of the huge ziggurat in the center of the city. From Daniel's place of prayer, he likely would have regularly heard a ritual where the drums beat as the parents carried their precious bundle up the stairs to be delivered to the Babylonian priest.[1]

The priest would then place the child in the arms of this heated bronze god. This statue was heated so hot that it would almost immediately fry the child to death. The drums helped mask the screams of the child being sacrificed.

Day after day, decade after decade, Daniel would pray, trying to worship the God of the universe while being in the midst of gods and goddesses of evil, hearing the screams of the innocent.

When we pray, we look toward heaven and the throne of Elohim. Obviously, we can't see the throne of God, but what do we, like Daniel, also feel around us? We see this world and the evil in it; we see wars, pestilence, and infant sacrifice. How can we worship a holy God when we are surrounded by evil? How did Daniel worship in the midst of such evil?

Many may reject Yahweh because of the evil in this world. They think that no good, perfect, and holy God can exist in a world filled with pain and suffering directed at even the most innocent. I think this is a valid question. How do we rectify this kind and degree of evil? How did Daniel and other biblical figures deal with evil?

The hard truth is that we do not have to know *why* evil exists. Daniel didn't know why; he didn't have all the answers. But what did Daniel do? He got on his knees three times a day and prayed.

Yes, it is a very evil world. And no, it does *not* make sense that God allows these evil things to occur. But we have to know that He is God. He is in control of all. And even the best of His people in history didn't have an answer for why evil things happen. They got on their knees and prayed.

Perhaps this is part of why evil exists. Both for Daniel and in our day, it is an ultimate test of strength, devotion, and reverence to the God Most High to trust that He knows best. Like it or not, being okay with this explanation and exhibiting trust in Yahweh is the only way to make it through our short time on this temporary planet.

It takes trust, it takes devotion, it takes faith.

For, even as faithful as we are to God, He is even more faithful to us. Psalm 100:5 reads, "For the LORD is good; His mercy is everlasting and His faithfulness is to all generations." Before we even knew God, he loved us. Jeremiah 1:5 reads, "Before I formed you in the womb I knew you, and before you were born I consecrated you; I have appointed you as a prophet to the nations." Having faith as demonstrated by God is not easy. In fact, for many it is a lifelong challenge. Throughout our lives, we are continually striving to fathom the love that God has for us. The world we live in is sinful. But dedicating ourselves to God and understanding His love more and more grants a deep solace that cannot be obtained from the world itself. As a child of God we can give up control, we don't have to have the answers, and we can trust God to have the ultimate right to rule over the earth.

CONNECTING THROUGH REFLECTIONS ON PRAYER

Linda

ℓ

How do you pray? Do you get on your hands and knees? Are your prayers habitually integrated into your day? Or do you pray at different times of the day? Prayer represents a deeply personal connection with God.

I am in awe of Daniel's prayer life. Three times a day—morning, noon, and evening, week after week, year after year, and decade after decade—praying for a nation trapped in evil, praying toward a temple that doesn't exist, on his knees, arms outstretched, worshipping God, petitioning his requests, praying for his people.

Daniel was a godly light in the dark city of Babylon. Yet, surrounded by evil, he continued to intercede for his people. Did he ever get tired, discouraged, or think, *God is not listening?* Did Daniel ever see the results of his prayers in his lifetime? As far as I can glean from the Scriptures, the answer was no for many of his prayers.

But we must keep praying, interceding, asking, and seeking God's face on behalf of those we love. To truly love someone, we must consistently pray for them, and we can tell that person we are praying for them. In an intergenerational connection, prayer is an important continuing step of the relationship. Praying for the future of the other is vital.

In Philippians 1:4 Paul reminds the Philippians that he is always praying for them; in Colossians 1:9 he reminds the Colossians that he continues to pray without ceasing for them; and in 1 Thessalonians 1:2 he reminds the Thessalonians he is praying for them.

Prayer passes through all generations. A small child can pray for a sick great-grandparent. This same grandparent can pray for their family even on their deathbed. Praying can happen while holding hands or over a long distance. Praying can be for a small child or the entire nation, for loved ones or someone you have never met.

When Kaitlyn asked me if I would say a prayer at her wedding, I immediately said yes. When I found out her mother was pregnant with Kaitlyn, I started praying for her. I prayed that she would be raised in a Christian home, learn about Christ at an early age, and walk in His way. When I found out that she was going to be a little girl, I started to pray for her husband to be, who turned out to be Elias, because we knew that someday this little girl would choose a husband. So we prayed that this man would also be raised in a Christian home, choose Christ, and walk in His way. I started praying for someone I didn't even know yet. I have prayed for the future spouses of all my grandchildren, that they would know the Lord, and that they together would create a Christian family that would be pleasing to the heavenly Father.

Prayer extends through all social classes and education levels. The Lord honors all sincere prayer; the prayer of a child ranks at the same level as the president of a nation. Our heavenly Father hears all of us. Pray together in your intergenerational relationship.

My children knew that my mom held her grandchildren up in prayer. When my daughter was in nurse's training, she frantically called me one day looking for her grandmother; she was going into a big test and she needed her grandmother to pray. She found her grandmother and asked her to pray, and she passed the test.

For Daniel, prayer was a vital aspect of his relationship with God. It did not matter that Daniel was in an idol-worshipping country, working for a king who did not serve the same God he did. Prayer was a testimony of Daniel's love for God. Likely, it also gave him peace.

In the same way, prayer can give us peace. We can lay the world's troubles at His feet and know that all is according to His will. In this way, prayer not only connects us with God but also connects us to each other.

We must strive to become a unified fellowship of children of God. When we pray for each other, we humble ourselves. We set aside our own ambitions and needs to lift up someone else. We should pray for each other across generations, and we should pray together. Through this fellowship, we find peace together in God.

Your prayers are treasured in heaven in golden vials, a beautiful aroma before the throne (Revelation 5:8). Pray with and for those you connect with in intergenerational communication. Be invested in their futures through prayer.

EIGHT
OTHER INTERESTING STORIES IN THE BOOK OF DANIEL

THE HUMBLING OF KING NEBBY

Linda

☙

K ing Nebuchadnezzar was the first king of Babylon with whom Daniel interacted. Nebuchadnezzar the Second was in Egypt, and after learning that his father died, he brought his army back through Jerusalem and kidnapped 10,832 citizens of Jerusalem and paraded them through the city of Babylon.

He was conqueror of many nations and destroyer of millions of people. He had absolute power and reign over his magnificent kingdom. He was feared by all. He was an idol worshiper. He also thought he was a god and worthy to be worshipped (Daniel 4). Just being near him could cost you your life. He ruled with absolute authority.

He was also one of the greatest architects ever known. His hanging gardens have been hailed as one of the seven wonders of the ancient world. The kingdom he built was magnificent. The Ishtar gate was the main entrance into the city of Babylon. A brick-for-brick replica is now displayed in Berlin's Pergamon Museum. The blue color of these bricks has been impossible to replicate. The tons of gold taken from the temple in Jerusalem would have made Babylon sparkle.

Nebuchadnezzar had a brilliant mind, wealth, power, and good health. He was also surrounded by the wise counsel of Daniel. He lacked nothing. There were many times Daniel was called upon to interpret Nebuchadnezzar's dreams and visions.

There is a strange story in Daniel 4:4–37, which you should read. Nebuchadnezzar was terrified again about a vision. He called in his entourage of soothsayers and, finally, Daniel to give an interpretation of the dream. He received a warning from God through Daniel. Nebuchadnezzar was supposed to stop sinning and show mercy to the poor. The warning was very intense. If he didn't stop sinning and show mercy to the poor, then he would be driven from men and banished to the field to eat grass like an ox.

If Daniel came to us and gave us two choices—eat grass like an ox for seven years or quit sinning and show mercy to the poor—I am sure all of us would choose the latter. Nebuchadnezzar, however, did not make the wise choice (Daniel 4:28–33). Twelve months later, when he opened his mouth, what did he say? "The king began speaking and was saying, 'Is this not Babylon the great, which I myself have built as a royal residence by the might of my power and for the honor of my majesty?'" (Daniel 4:29–30). He got caught up in his pride and rejected God. The chapter says that while he was still speaking, he was driven from men and into the field.

I would love to have been in the palace when Nebuchadnezzar was first affected. Can you imagine the scene? What were his advisors going to do with this man? Now imagine you have close ties to the king of Babylon. He was an absolute despot ruler. He demanded power, evil, and absolute sovereignty. If he did not like you, you died a painful death. Remember the furnace? When the king went crazy, did those in charge call Daniel? I would have.

Nebuchadnezzar's fall was spectacular and legendary. He lost his health, mental stability, empire, power, kingship over men, and palace. Looking on this reversal of fortune, I cannot imagine him falling lower than this. God showed us with this example that He and only He is in control of everything. He will not tolerate prideful boasts and will humble even kings.

Nebuchadnezzar roamed the field eating grass like an ox for seven years. This is a real psychological condition called boanthropy where a man actually thinks that he is an ox. We studied it very briefly in nurse's training.

We don't know much about Nebuchadnezzar's physical traits, but he was an incredibly powerful ruler. Yet Nebuchadnezzar, at the command of Elohim, was in the field eating grass like an ox for seven years. Why didn't his foes just kill him as he was roaming around the pasture defenseless? The answer lies in the belief at the time that if you kill an insane man, the evil spirit inside the person would jump out into you. They were very reluctant to kill, harm, or injure anyone who was acting strangely. They left him alone.

But when Nebuchadnezzar became mad, whose bright idea was it to take him to the field? All the palace was probably pacing around, and several might have suggested, "Let's shut him up in the palace." Some might have said, "No, the dungeon will be more controlled and safer." Who said, "Take him to the field with cows and sheep and pigs so he can eat grass like an ox"? Might I suggest that Daniel had a part in this plan? Daniel said that the Lord of the universe decreed that Nebuchadnezzar go to the field for seven years.

When evil kings became mad, no one banished them to a field with grass. I am thinking of the Roman Caesars Caligula and Nero in particular, but there are many others who probably should have been banished with the oxen. This fate of Nebuchadnezzar's was divine intervention. If you actually liked the king and were part of his inner circle, this would have been extremely upsetting. Did his citizens and slaves come to see what God had done? Was there fear in the kingdom toward the God of Daniel? If the powerful king could be taken down, what about anyone and their family? Let me also suggest that this episode was a great evangelistic tool for Daniel to show the Lord's power.

When he was in the field, who fed Nebuchadnezzar? Man cannot live by grass alone, at least not for seven years. Who gave him water? Or protected him from the beasts of the field and poisonous mushrooms? Who ran his kingdom for seven years? I believe the answer to these questions is Daniel.

After seven years, just as prophesied, Nebuchadnezzar lifted his eyes to heaven and praised and worshipped the Most High

God. He returned to his kingdom, and increased power and majesty were given to him (Daniel 4:34–37). The last time we see Nebuchadnezzar, he is praising the everlasting God of the universe.

The number seven is a very prominent number throughout the Bible that refers to completion. It is a prophetic number, and it often marks periods of time in God's eyes. It all ties back to the Sabbath, or *Shabbat* in Hebrew. This topic is a very long study in itself, but it is important to know that in remembrance of the Sabbath (working six days and resting on the seventh) the Israelites were called to set their slaves free every seven years. At the very least it was to be an option for those slaves.

I am reminded of this concept while reading this story about Nebuchadnezzar where he was enslaved in his own way for seven years. After those years were complete, Yahweh's mercy allowed him to be released from his state, and he was given power and authority again to praise Yahweh and proclaim His name under his rule. It is an interesting parallel to our Savior Yeshua. We were a slave to our sin, but because of His mercy we have been set free, forgiven, and are able to praise His name.

Another kind of biblical sabbath applies to the land of Israel. It is partly because of Israel's disobedience in regard to the sabbath of the land that Jerusalem was destroyed and the people carried off to Babylon.

At the time of Daniel, Israel did not celebrate the sabbath year of rest for the land. Most people are familiar with the Sabbath *day* of rest, but the sabbath *year* of rest for the land is less common knowledge. Every seven years there was a "set-aside" year where no plowing or planting was to be done. Everything that grew voluntarily was not to be sold. Part of the crops that grew on their own, including grapes from vineyards, barley, wheat, and soybeans from fields, were to be given away to the poor, widowed, and orphaned. I am in awe of this concept.

The sabbath for the land is called the Shmita year, which means release or remission. According to the Torah, the land was to rest the full duration of the seventh year. However, the people in Jerusalem and surrounding area had gone 490 years without observing the sabbath law of the land. Then, with captivity, the land rested seventy years while the people were in Babylon.

The number of years of exile equaled the number of years that the Shmita was not observed. In other words, 490 (the number of years the sabbath was ignored) divided by seven (every seventh year was supposed to be a sabbath year) equals seventy (the number of years Israel was forced to rest the land, so to speak, while they were in captivity). The God of the universe is in absolute control of the land, and its people belong to Him.

I live in an agricultural area, and this idea of a sabbath year rest for the land is absolutely foreign to me. The Midwest feeds the cities, states, nation, and world with our corn, soybeans, wheat, etc. Could we take a whole year off and just see what comes up? Elohim says that we can and benefit greatly from this decision. What do you say, dear reader?

THE WRITING ON THE WALL

Linda

❦

Read chapter 5 of Daniel, where we see another weird story. Nebuchadnezzar had died, and now the kingdom inside the walls of Babylon was ruled by Belshazzar, who was Nebuchadnezzar's grandson. Belshazzar made a great feast for one thousand of his nearest and dearest lords—and they were very drunk. The king commanded that they bring out the gold and silver vessels that were taken from the temple of the Lord in Jerusalem so that his princes, wives, and concubines could drink out of them and toast and praise the gods of gold, silver, brass, iron, wood, and stone.

So, the king toasted the idol gods of gold, silver, brass, iron, wood, and stone with the cups that were dedicated to the God of the universe. I probably don't have to tell you—the king was very foolish. Did he not remember the incident with Nebuchadnezzar where God made him roam the pasture for seven years? In Daniel 5:22 we learn that Belshazzar did indeed know what had happened to Nebuchadnezzar and still chose to rebel. He had no fear of the Lord.

In Daniel 5 a hand appeared and wrote on the wall of the banquet hall: "Menē, Menē, Tekēl, Upharsin" (Daniel 5:25).

Josephus, the ancient historian, said that "he saw a hand proceed out of the wall and writing upon the wall certain syllables."[1] Of course, Daniel was brought in to interpret the writing. These words essentially mean, "You have been weighed and found deficient."

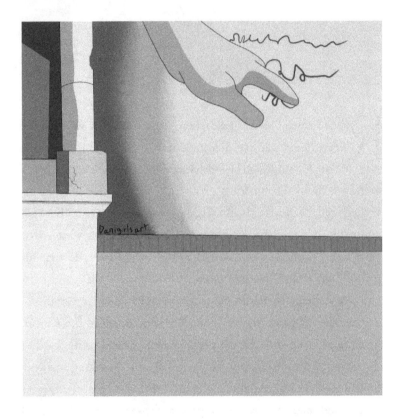

The king did not believe that his kingdom would be destroyed. His city, Babylon, was surrounded by a huge impenetrable wall, and there was enough food inside the city to last for many years. However, that night Darius the Mede diverted the waters of the Euphrates, and his army passed through a tunnel under the city.

Babylon surrendered without even a battle, the king was killed, and again Daniel was placed second in command (Daniel 6:1–3). The date that King Belshazzar was killed and the palace stormed was October 16 in 539 BC.[2]

Is it possible that the hand of God in Daniel was Yeshua's? If this is the case, it is not hard to see the connection between the incident in Daniel and another time the hand of God the Son is seen writing.

In John 8:1–11 the scribes and pharisees brought a woman caught in the act of adultery before Yeshua. But where is the man with whom she was caught? Leviticus 20:10 states that both the man and the woman are to be brought forward and stoned after thorough evidence has been given. This was likely a test with which the scribes and Pharisees tried to trick Yeshua.

Roman law prohibited the Jews from their own use of capital punishment. The Romans killed a lot of people, but others were not permitted to stone or kill anyone.

If Yeshua would have said, "Yes, stone her," then Rome would have killed the accusers; if Yeshua would have said, "No," then he would have been going against the Torah. He was between a rock and a hard place. I believe that in response, when He bent to write on the ground, He wrote "Menē, Menē, Tekēl, Upharsin" in the dust. The older, wiser men recognized the hand of God from the story in Daniel and left first, followed by the younger men.

If I am right in this speculation, the meaning of "Menē, Menē, Tekēl, Upharsin" becomes richer for us. Daniel 5 interprets these words for us: "This is the interpretation of the message: 'Menē'— God has numbered your kingdom and put an end to it. 'Tekēl'—

you have been weighed on the scales and found deficient" (Daniel 5:26–27).

When the men brought the woman to Jesus, they had counted her sins and found her guilty. However, as Jesus points out, everyone in that crowd had been found guilty of sin in their lives. Jesus initiated a challenge. He gave permission to throw a stone barring one condition: you must never have sinned. Rightfully so, nobody could look him in the eye and answer in the affirmative. "All have sinned and fall short of the glory of God" (Romans 3:23). I speculate that Jesus then began to write this phrase in the dirt: "You have been weighed and found deficient."

Unfortunately, we can relate with the crowd; we have all sinned in our lives. However, Jesus has an answer. With the sacrifice of His life for our sins, we are offered forgiveness, grace, and mercy (Ephesians 1:7). We do not need to cast stones at one another. Instead, we can be united in our acceptance of God's love and mercy.

GOLD, FRANKINCENSE, AND MYRRH

Linda

❧

I s there a connection between Daniel in 600 BC and the Messiah in AD 3? I believe Daniel taught the prophecies of Jeremiah, Micah, and others to the Babylonian magi. I believe that he also taught them the Torah and that this knowledge was passed down generation after generation, century after century until a star appeared.

Open your Bibles and read Matthew 2:1–16.

John H. Hopkins Jr. wrote a wonderful hymn in 1857. He was a music teacher and composer through the horrific years of the Civil War (1860–1865).

"We Three Kings"

We three kings of Orient are;
Bearing gifts we traverse afar.
Field and fountain, moor and mountain,
Following yonder star.

O, star of wonder, star of night,
Star with royal beauty bright,
Westward leading, still proceeding,
Guide us to Thy perfect light.

Though that was just the first verse, I remember singing that hymn as a child and dreaming of those regal men on camels traveling to see the Messiah. I have collected many nativity sets throughout the years and have them displayed throughout my house. My most precious set was bought by my daughter in Oberammergau, Germany, while her husband was stationed in the Netherlands. In every complete set, there are three kings with at least one camel. One of my sets has a king riding on an elephant—weird. Another set has a king riding on a horse. Neither the elephant nor the horse would have been practical for the terrain they would have traveled. Camels, which are called "ships of the desert," were the perfect means of transportation. They can go weeks without water and can carry enormous loads of cargo as well as humans on their backs. The kings probably came on camels. However, (1) were they kings, (2) were there only three, and (3) were they from the Orient?

Let's tackle question number one. Were they kings? Matthew 2:1–12 records this event. The term here is not kings, but magi. The word *magi* means "wise men," so they themselves were not kings.

Matthew 2:2 states that they "saw His star in the east." They were probably well versed in astronomy and knowledge of the planets, stars, and patterns in the sky. They realized there was a star whose presence announced the arrival of a King, and they wanted to find this special King in order to worship Him.

Question number two: were there only three? We know the Bible records that they brought three gifts: gold, frankincense, and myrrh. Maybe this is why it was always assumed that there must have been three people who brought the three gifts, but we really do not know how many there were. I personally believe that this was an army of men that was approaching Jerusalem unannounced. The reason for this belief is based in two small words in Matthew 2:3: "troubled" and "all."

King Herod was said to be troubled, which means trembling with fear. King Herod would not have trembled over three tired men riding camels ladened with gold, frankincense, and myrrh. Knowing some of the history of Herod, I assume he would have just had them killed and swiped their treasures. However, an army of men coming from the east to worship a new king would have troubled Herod greatly.

All the men named Herod found in biblical history were evil, but this one in Matthew 2 was particularly bad. According to Josephus, he killed several of his own sons, a wife, a mother-in-law, a brother-in-law, and hundreds, maybe thousands, of others. He also killed the male children two years old and younger living in Bethlehem after the magi left Jerusalem. This is documented in Scripture in Matthew 2:16–18. Thus, Herod would certainly not have trembled at the approach of three tired men on camels. The people would have trembled at a large army since they knew the story of the Babylonians who came to Jerusalem in 605 BC with their armies, conquered the people, and took them into slavery. The Babylonian army also came from the east as the magi did.

Question number three: were they from the Orient? Scripture states that they were from east of Jerusalem (Matthew 2:1). I believe they were from Babylon, which was one of the largest cities to the east of Jerusalem. Additionally, there was a long-standing connection between the cities because of their intertwined pasts we have discussed so prominently in this book.

Babylon was a long journey, about a thousand miles one way. To equip an army with food and water to travel over rugged terrain would have been an undertaking of great magnitude. It truly shows determination and a faith that could move mountains.

How did they know about the King of kings? How did they know He was human, born Jewish in Bethlehem? Why did they question this particular star and immediately associate it with the King of the universe? Could Daniel be the reason? Is it possible that these events were known about ahead of time because of the influence of Daniel and his understanding of prophecies to come?

Possible answers to these questions are why I think that the magi were from Babylon. Let's look at Daniel 1:1–7. In 605 BC when King Nebuchadnezzar of Babylon came to Jerusalem in three waves of terror, we know that Daniel was taken. Also, riches of the temple were stolen, including the most priceless treasures of all—the ancient manuscripts. Some of these ancient manuscripts have been preserved in our Old Testament as the Torah. They tell of the coming King Messiah, of Him being Jewish and born in Bethlehem. They tell of Him being Lord of Lords and King of kings, forever reigning, as well as being the sacrificial Lamb for our sins.

The wise men of Babylon likely would have read and studied these manuscripts and would certainly have known about Daniel and his great wealth of knowledge. Additionally, Daniel's status in the king's council would have provided lots of material wealth. Daniel had no family of his own to pass his enormous wealth on to.

At the time of Yeshua's birth, Daniel had been dead for more than five hundred years, but the prophecies contained in those manuscripts, the knowledge Daniel possessed, and his material inheritance had been passed down for centuries until the point in time when everything was set into motion for Yeshua to come to Earth.

So, when the magi saw the star and the signs in the sky, they were filled with awe and wonder, and they knew the time had come. They were to be the ones to carry forth the plan of delivering treasures to Daniel's Messiah and worshipping Him as such.

As recorded in Matthew 2:2, the magi said, "We saw His star in the east and have come to worship Him." Psalms 19:1 says, "The heavens tell of the glory of God; and their expanse declares the work of His hands." God foretold the Messiah's coming in the stars to those who knew how to read them.

The magi's mission was to travel over a thousand miles on camels, through arduous terrain, with all the challenges that accompany such a journey. They gathered armies and enough supplies together for a long journey, along with the gifts for this precious child.

It is amazing that Daniel holds this connection to the Messiah. Even though Daniel's life was filled with challenges, his knowledge and wealth were passed down for generations to ultimately finance Yeshua's escape to Egypt and to safety. Wow! This kind of planning can only be accomplished by Yahweh Himself.

CONCLUSION

Linda

We need to end on a happy note; we can't leave these precious kids in Babylon forever. Psalm 126 is one of ten psalms that are called the psalms of ascent. It is sung every year in worship to the Lord as the Israelites ascend (or go up) to Jerusalem. After captivity they were free from Babylon's enslavement, and singing joyfully, they ascended the hill.

> When the LORD brought back the captives of Zion,
> We were like those who dream.
> Then our mouth was filled with laughter
> And our tongue with joyful shouting;
> Then they said among the nations,
> "The LORD has done great things for them."
> The LORD has done great things for us;
> We are joyful.
>
> Restore our fortunes, LORD,
> As the streams in the South.
> Those who sow in tears shall harvest with joyful shouting.

One who goes here and there weeping, carrying his
    bag of seed,
Shall indeed come again with a shout of joy,
bringing his sheaves with him. (Psalm 126)

The omnipotent, omniscient, omnipresent, supreme ruler, sustainer, merciful, loving, Most High, eternal Creator of the universe, Yahweh, has placed the knowledge of eternity in our heart and in our mind. Through His Word we know that we do not belong here on this earth, and we are just passing through. So as Christians we wait. Beth Moore once said that the storm is not yet here, but we hear a distant thunder. All of us who study prophecy can hear a distant thunder and some of us see flashes of lightning. He is coming—soon.

The wait seems long, but we read many times in the Scriptures that the famous followers of the Lord also waited. Joseph waited in prison two years before Pharaoh needed someone to interpret a dream (Genesis 41). Jacob worked seven long years for his bride Rachel, who then waited year after year for a son (Genesis 30). Abraham's wife, Sarah, was ninety years old before her promised child was born (Genesis 21), and Hannah was barren and finally given a child after a visit to the temple in Jerusalem (1 Samuel 1–2).

Israel waited for deliverance in Egypt, for the promise of the Lord. The Israelites wandered forty years for a glimpse of the promised land. Paul spent time bouncing from one prison to the next, spending the final years of his life under Roman arrest, waiting to be martyred. Daniel waited decades in between visions and prophecies, always looking toward his beloved homeland, Jerusalem. We are waiting also. We know with assurance that

Messiah will come again, so we wait. We study Scripture and tell our family, friends, and others to look up because redemption draws near (Luke 21:28).

Daniel saw visions and angels many times in his life. At the very end of the book of Daniel, we see Daniel in the presence of two angel messengers. Prophecy was given to Daniel about the end of the age, and he was told that he would die but also rise from the dead at the last days.

Read Daniel 12. I told you in the beginning of this book that I would not go into detail about the prophecies given by the Lord to Daniel. However, in Daniel 12 we have a revelation of the end times that needs to be mentioned.

"Now at that time Michael, the great prince who stands guard over the sons of your people, will arise. And there will be a time of distress such as never occurred since there was a nation until that time; and at that time your people, everyone who is found written in the book, will be rescued" (Daniel 12:1).

Michael is the angel who protects the Jewish people. In the future there shall be a time of distress as has never occurred *since* there was a *nation*. The nation of Israel was founded May 12, 1948. This prophecy is talking about distress even greater than the Holocaust. But the people whose names are found written in the Book of Life will be rescued.

"And those who have insight will shine like the glow of the expanse of heaven, and those who lead the many to righteousness, like the stars forever and ever" (Daniel 12:3).

At the time spoken of in this section of Daniel, wise men and women will shine, and those who turn many to righteousness will live forever. As Christians and believers in Yahweh, we are to worship and celebrate Elohim, and Yeshua, and make disciples. Part of evangelism is guiding others toward the Savior, a feat that can only be accomplished in a humble way, with the knowledge of one's own sins, and through the guidance of the Holy Spirit.

"But as for you, Daniel, keep these words secret and seal up the book until the end of time; many will roam about, and knowledge will increase" (Daniel 12:4).

When I was growing up, except for members of my family who fought in WWI or WWII or a rich uncle, I knew no one who had left the country for business or pleasure. Presently, a lot of people I know have been out of the continental United States. Flying or driving to parts unknown is not *that* big of a deal anymore.

As we can see in Daniel 12:4, knowledge will increase in the end times. With the computer, internet, and everything else, knowledge is exploding. These are signs of the end. So, when is "the end"? We have to go to Yeshua's words in Matthew 24:14. It will be after the gospel (Word of Yeshua) is preached in all the world unto all nations. We are responsible for getting the Word out.

"But as for me, I heard but did not understand; so I said, 'My lord, what will be the outcome of these events?' And he said, 'Go your way, Daniel, for these words will be kept secret and sealed up until the end time'" (Daniel 12:8–9).

Daniel did not understand the prophecy and was told that the meaning of the prophetic Word would be revealed at the end of time. At that time, the righteous will be given understanding. I believe this prophecy is starting to unfold. Authors with great insight are writing best-sellers about this future event. However, you do not need to be brilliant teachers, theologians, or rabbis to interpret the Word. You just need to take the time to read and study the Word for yourself. The Holy Spirit will give you needed understanding.

Out of all the people who walked away from Jerusalem and actually made it to Babylon, how many examples of absolute commitment to the Lord do we have besides the four? I have no idea. It may have only been four.

I have four grandchildren the age of Daniel when he was taken to Babylon. Would they be strong enough to travel the distance? Would they fail under pressure? Would they refuse the king's food, refuse to worship the idols, and refuse to abandon their prayer to Yahweh? Would they walk to the furnace? I like to think that they would, but would they?

Would *I* walk to the furnace? You can destroy a rock of granite two ways: one is by dynamite, and another is by a slow drip of water. I think the Christians in our nation are experiencing a slow drip. Slowly, slowly, our Christian absolutes are challenged, and we are becoming like the world. Like the church in Ephesus (Revelation 2:1–7), we have lost our first love. Many of our churches have become country clubs minus the golf course. In some traditions there is limited accountability for preaching against sin and toward righteousness. We know what is right, for the Lord has given all of us a conscience and His Word. We need to stop the drip!

The four stood up against the powers and rulers, and according to Daniel 1:17–20, they were given knowledge and skill in all learning and wisdom, ten times better than all the so-called wise men of the kingdom. There are blessings in following the Lord. We will still have trouble and pain because we have to live here, but we have an advocate in heaven who is Yeshua.

If there is only one message we can take away from the wonderful book of Daniel, it is to trust our Lord.

Trust Him in the absolute devastation and utter destruction of your life and the people and family around you.

Trust Him to provide food and shelter and physical needs.

Trust Him to provide people to walk alongside you.

Trust Him to know the future, and believe that He has your best interest and the welfare of your family in mind.

Trust Him in the lions' den.

Trust Him in the fiery furnace.

Trust Him when evil leaders and people are in control.

Trust Him with your very life and eternity.

Trust Him to have everything under control. Even if it doesn't feel that way at times.

Trust Him as Daniel did.

Yahweh was the true origin of Daniel's strength. Daniel had faith and trust that God would provide for him. That God was who He said He was. That God would provide him with everything listed above.

We need to know that His Word is truth, it has been passed down for millennia, and it is relevant for our day. Elohim, Yeshua, and Holy Spirit are in control of the future in all things.

There will eventually be shalom in this world because evil will be defeated and the kingdom of Yahweh will reign. Daniel likely had no idea what influence he would have. That twenty-five-hundred plus years later, we would be studying him and reading what he wrote.

I think Daniel is the greatest prophet who ever lived besides, of course, Yeshua the Son. I can't be a Daniel, and you probably can't either. But who fed him and his friends when they were teenagers and young adults? My grandsons are eating machines. Austin has three breakfasts before lunch; he just stands in front of a full refrigerator contemplating what to devour next. Who fills the refrigerator over and over again? Who picked up Daniel's robe off the floor, mended it, and washed it? Who made his bed and dusted the ancient scrolls? Who cleaned his room and took care of his bed chamber pot?

These are the unsung heroes; these could be me, or they could be you for the next generation. This work does not go unnoticed in the heavenly places. I predict when we have a roll call upstairs, there will be countless people who were helpers of many, including the prophets, and even the Son of our heavenly Father. These are the Marthas. These are the behind-the-scenes workers for the kingdom. Hang in there and praise your heavenly Father. Your work may not be noticed on Earth, but it is certainly noticed by our Father in heaven, His Son, and the angels.

I picked up my twin grandsons from Sunday school once when they were about three years old, and I asked them what they had learned.

Austin said with huge eyes, "God is everywhere."

Several days later, both boys were playing outside with fresh snow on the ground, and the last thing their mommy told them was not to play by the egress window or else they would fall in. Guess how many minutes before one boy fell in? It was about five minutes. It was Austin, and he started screaming hysterically trying to climb out but failing to do so. Ethan ran for help. By the time their mommy had arrived, Austin was bright red from screaming and had lost a boot attempting to climb out.

He was screaming, "I was all alone, I was all alone."

Ethan said, "You weren't alone, Austin. God was with you."

I want to tell you, dear reader, when you are caught in a snow-packed egress window and are screaming and have lost a boot from trying to claw your way out, God is with you and an "Ethan" will run for help.

Daniel was all alone many times in his life, but he diligently prayed three times a day facing a temple he would never see again. The temple represents the presence of Yahweh, the Elohim of the universe. Daniel also knew that this supreme being was with him always and was everywhere. Even in Babylon and even in a lions' den.

Throughout this book we have encouraged the formation of intergenerational connections, and we hope you will seek out intergenerational communication, dear reader. I truly think that there is so much to learn from these kinds of conversations. By forming connections with others through an understanding of different contexts and backgrounds, joining in community through common action, building a foundation of love and acceptance, challenging each other to grow and learn, and by investing in the futures of each other, we are able to create deeper connections that lead many to Yahweh across many generations.

I hope generations after Generation Z (what can they possibly be called?) will read this and know that their great-great-great-grandma loved Elohim and wants all her descendants to live forever with her in heaven someday.

Maranatha!

KAITLYN'S FINAL REFLECTION

The process of writing this book has presented many challenges, triumphs, and times of reflection.

When my grandma first told me about the idea of writing about Daniel, a young man who was fifteen or sixteen when he went through great trauma, I had no clue it would turn into a multiyear project.

I laugh about it now, but at first I was just going to help turn her written scribbles into a typed document. I can't imagine her trying to type on a computer (she has a hard enough time turning it on). I had helped her type other Bible studies in the past, and it was usually a one- or two-day procedure that created four- or five-page mini Bible studies.

But, like for my grandma, Daniel captured me. His story amazed me. It was a different telling of the same story I thought I knew, but somehow this was so much more. It was a different perspective. A more human perspective. I can honestly say that my perception of *all* biblical figures has been altered by my grandma's insights.

I remember sitting down with her to make our first outline (of many). I don't think she quite understood the point of the outline at that time. She is an extremely talented storyteller, a quality I wish I had, but her thoughts in writing tend to be a little more scattered than organized and linear. She wanted to start writing, I wanted an outline, and she looked at me like, "Why?"

"This is a book now, Grandma. It's a book."

She later told me she didn't realize how big of an idea it was until the moment I told her it was a book. The ideas exploded from there.

My grandma taught me how to really study. We would start off each day of work on this book with prayer. We would ask Elohim to guide us, protect us, and allow us to put our own worries aside to have the clarity to say what He wanted us to say. I am so very thankful for this guidance.

My life has completely changed while writing this book. I wanted to be a doctor; now I have graduated with a psychology degree and plan to teach. My walk with God was stagnant; now He has led me to feel an explosion of growth and future purpose. Where I was clueless, my passion for teaching, communication, and deepening relationships has become clear. My grandma and I were close, but now we are so much closer.

We went into this project with the mind-set of melding the perspectives of multiple generations. We are leaving this project completely changed by the process and with the desire for others to develop similar relationships. Yahweh's people are supposed to be in community with each other. We are not designed to be on our own separate islands all the time.

I am not saying that it is possible for everyone to have the kind of awakening experience that I had, but I think the level of understanding we developed through conversations about Yahweh, His Word, our joys and fears, purpose, life and death, and how to love others will impact us forever—as will be true for everyone who chooses to pursue a similar intergenerational connection.

I encourage you, dear reader, to strive for this. The quote referenced at the beginning of the book, "What would happen if the people who see only the past and the people who see only the future were to turn around and face each other?" is a perfect way for generations of people to envision growth, a growth we all can strive for.

LINDA'S FINAL REFLECTION

I have been teaching Bible studies for forty years, and Kaitlyn is the smartest person who has ever sat across from me. Our studies together have given me great joy. I could study with her for years and not grow tired. I am amazed by new technology and frustrated. The saying "You can't teach an old dog new tricks" applies here. She can find information in minutes that would have taken me hours, if ever, to find. She has such great ideas and writing skills; she takes my disjointed sentences and makes them readable and understandable, and I almost sound smart. I am thankful.

This manuscript has been a multiyear undertaking. The Lord spoke to us in so many ways. We are blessed. Kaitlyn is a truly remarkable young lady. Her life now is like Daniel's—that of a Christian surrounded by unbelievers. Her life may be like Jeremiah in the future—one disaster after another. Whatever happens, I know the Lord will be in control of everything.

It's time now to pass the baton like Paul did to Timothy.

To a thousand generations.

"Know therefore that the LORD your God, He is God,
the faithful God, who keeps His covenant and His
faithfulness to a thousand generations for those who
love Him and keep His commandments."

(Deuteronomy 7:9)

STUDY AND DISCUSSION QUESTIONS

1. The false gods of Babylon could do nothing. They were just stone and wood; they had no power. For King Darius to ask Daniel whether his God was able to deliver him from the lions was a step forward in Darius knowing the one true God. For Darius, the false gods of his culture may have been roadblocks to a faith in Yahweh. What is a false god? What false gods exist in our culture today?

2. Daniel went down, down, and lower down into the lions' den, a "unique" prayer closet. Another Old Testament prophet who also went down, down, down into a unique prayer closet was Jonah. This prophet was a statesman on top of the world until God asked him to evangelize the hated Ninevites. Jonah ran from God, went down to Joppa, down into a ship, down into

the belly of a fish, and down into the sea (Jonah 1:3). In the belly of a fish Jonah looked up and prayed, and the fish came up to the surface to vomit him from its mouth. Do you have a "prayer closet" or space where you can go away to read, hear, and study the Word of God and pray, away from everything else? If not, how can you implement this practice?

3. Have you ever been in a pit so deep (physically, mentally, or spiritually) that the only thing you could do is look up? This pit might have been dug by you or someone else who pushed you into it. David had this problem, which he wrote about in Psalm 35:7–8. Jeremiah also had the same problem (Jeremiah18:19–23). There is no pit that is too deep for God. He will always be with you. Are you in your own lions' den now? Have you been in a lions' den in the past? Reflect on actions you can take to remain grounded in God as Daniel did in his lions' den.

4. Has pride ever gotten you into a lot of trouble like King Darius
    or the other kings found in the book of Daniel? Look up Micah
    6:8. What is our responsibility as followers of Elohim? What
    are we to do?

5. Think back to when you were fifteen to nineteen years old.
    How would you have handled what Jeremiah went through? In
    my reflection, I'd say, "Yikes! Likely not very well."

6. Jeremiah asks a question in Jeremiah 5:30–31. Look this up
    in your Bible. The first adjective is translated as "astonishing,"
    from the Hebrew word *shammah*, but some translations have
    "appalling" or "shocking." What is the question, and how
    would you answer it?

7. As Americans we live in a nation where, thankfully, we can worship and own a Bible without being afraid of death. We cannot fall asleep now; we must be alert because, as 1 Peter 5:8 tells us, "Your adversary, the devil, prowls around like a roaring lion, seeking someone to devour." What are some tangible ways you can further the kingdom of the Lord?

8. As we consider the challenges that Daniel had as a youth, think about the teenagers of today. What are some similarities and differences between these two groups separated by thousands of years?

9. Nebuchadnezzar's pride got him in a lot of trouble with God. What are some tangible ways you grow from the knowledge that God will humble even a king?

10. Have you ever achieved a very difficult goal in your life, school, or business, and stood back and said, "Look at what I have done," never praising the heavenly Father for helping you along the way and allowing you to accomplish this great feat? I will admit that this is something I have done. When we get to heaven, we will probably see all the help we have had along the way in our life. The near misses of destruction and of failure. List and reflect on a few of the blessings you have received in your life.

11. What other Old Testament characters fell dramatically, from the top of the world to the bottom? Look up the Old Testament book of Job. Read Job 1–2:10. What did Job lose? What did Job gain in the end?

12. Look up Proverbs 1:7, 9:10, and 31:30. Define the word *fear*.
    Our God is the sovereign ruler of the universe; we should
    respect and honor Him. Did Belshazzar fear God? Do you fear
    God? What does fearing God look like?

ACKNOWLEDGMENTS

Thank you to Suzanne Phinney for clarifying our messy thoughts, helping with research, and being an amazing encouragement throughout the process.

Thank you to Elias Dallmann for his support and thoughts throughout the book.

Thank you to Brenda Herzinger and Dr. Elvin Brown for editorial corrections.

Thank you to the Illumify team, especially Mike Klassen, Jen Clark, Deb Hall, Lisa Hawker, and Geoff Stone for their desire to make this book the best it could be.

Thank you to the NWU Bible study group, especially Megan, for your valuable generational input.

And thank you to all others, especially Glenn Dallmann, who read and reread and re-reread the many drafts of this project. Your critique was invaluable.

ABOUT THE AUTHORS

LINDA BROWN is a child of Elohim, wife, mother of three daughters, mother-in-law of three sons, and grandmother of eight exceptional grandchildren.

She has an RN degree from Bishop Clarkson Memorial Hospital (Omaha, Nebraska), which she earned in 1968.

She is a Precept Ministry (Kay and David Arthur) certified teacher with over forty years of experience teaching women's Bible studies, mostly using original material.

She also "attempts" to play bridge and golf.

KAITLYN DALLMANN is a child of Elohim. Her immediate family—her husband, Elias, and puppy, Daisy—in addition to her father, mother, and twin brothers, are a large part of her life and a strong source of encouragement.

She graduated from Nebraska Wesleyan University with a bachelor of science degree in psychology. She plans to attend graduate school for a master's degree and then teach.

She enjoys playing tennis, watching movies with friends, and spoiling her little puppy.

NOTES

Introduction

1   Paul H. Wright, *Heart of the Holy Land: 40 Reflections on Scripture and Place* (Peabody, MA: Rose Publishing, 2020), 213.

Chapter One: Vital Information

1   Flavius Josephus, *The New Complete Works of Josephus,* rev. and expanded ed., trans. William Whiston (Grand Rapids, MI: Kregel Publications, 1999), 56–57.

2   *King James Study Bible,* full color ed. (Nashville, TN: Thomas Nelson, 2017).

3   Padraic Colum, "Semiramis," in *World Book Encyclopedia*, v. 17 (1984), 235.

4   Robert J. Lenardon, "Zeus," in *World Book Encyclopedia*, v. 21 (1984), 496.

5   Nicola Stow, "Inside Abandoned Babylon Built by Saddam Hussein Who Thought He Was Reincarnation of Ancient King Nebuchadnezzar, The U.S. Sun, the-sun.com, December 3, 2019, https://www.the-sun.com/news/us-news/116748/inside-abandoned-babylon-built-by-saddam-hussein-who-thought-he-was-reincarnation-of-ancient-king-nebuchadnezzar/.

6   Amber K. Worthington, Jon F. Nussbaum, and Mark J. Bergstrom, "Intergenerational Communication, Oxford Bibliographies, November 29, 2018, www.oxfordbibliographies.com/display/document/obo-9780199756841/obo-9780199756841-0217.xml.

Chapter Two: Daniel Had Strength

1   John MacArthur, The MacArthur Study Bible – New King James Version, 2nd ed. (Nashville, TN: Thomas Nelson, 2019), 1040.

2   Flavius Josephus, *The New Complete Works of Josephus*, rev. and expanded ed., trans. William Whiston (Grand Rapids, MI: Kregel Publications, 1999), 345–47.

3   Flavius Josephus, 345.

4   Flavius Josephus, 345.

Chapter Five: Daniel Had Devotion

1   King James Study Bible (Nashville, TN: Holman, 2012), 1409.

2   Peter Hong, "'But If Not': How Biblical Literacy Jolted Civilian Brits Into Action at Dunkirk," *The Stream*, August 12, 2017, https://stream.org/but-if-not-biblical-literacy/.

Chapter Seven: Daniel Had Prayer

1   John MacArthur, The MacArthur Study Bible – New King James Version, 2nd ed. (Nashville, TN: Thomas Nelson, 2019), 501.

Chapter Eight: Other Interesting Stories in the Book of Daniel

1   Flavius Josephus, *The New Complete Works of Josephus*, rev. and expanded ed., trans. William Whiston (Grand Rapids, MI: Kregel Publications, 1999), 354.

2   John MacArthur, The MacArthur Study Bible – New King James Version, second ed. (Nashville, TN: Thomas Nelson, 2019), 1109.

Printed in the USA
CPSIA information can be obtained
at www.ICGtesting.com
BVHW041242170823
668636BV00004B/12